THE BASICS OF FINANCIAL EDUCATION

A Guide for Beginners on How to Grow the Right Skills for Financial Freedom and Economic Independence. Improve Your Business Position in Finance and Work.

The Basics of Financial Education

The Basics of Financial Education

© Copyright 2023 - All rights reserved.

The contents of this book may not be reproduced, duplicated or transmitted without the direct written permission of the author or publisher.

In no event shall any legal fault or liability be held against the publisher, or author, for any damages, repairs, or monetary losses because of the information contained in this book. Directly or indirectly.

Legal notes:

This book is copyrighted. This book is for personal use only. You may not modify, distribute, sell, use, quote, or paraphrase any part, or the content within this book, without the consent of the author or publisher.

Disclaimer notice:

Please note that the information contained in this document is for educational and entertainment purposes only. All efforts have been made to present accurate, up-to-date, and reliable and complete information. No warranty of any kind is stated or implied. Readers acknowledge that the author is not engaged in providing legal, financial, medical, or professional advice. The content within this book has been derived from various sources. Please consult a licensed professional before attempting the techniques described in this book.

By reading this document, the reader agrees that in no event shall the author be liable for any loss, direct or indirect, they suffer as a result of the use of information contained within this document, including, but not limited to, errors, omissions, or inaccuracies.

The Basics of Financial Education

The Basics of Financial Education

Introduction

Chapter 1 - Reading and Interpreting Events in Our Favor
Chapter 2 – Financial Education
Chapter 3 – Self-Training "Shock"
Chapter 4 - Economy and Investment
Chapter 5 - Educational Context
Chapter 6 - Informational Context
Chapter 7 - Economic Context
Chapter 8 - Future Scenarios and Digitization
Chapter 9 - Money and Currency
Chapter 10 - Inflation and Hyperinflation
Chapter 11 - New Forms of Warfare
Chapter 12 - Crisis as Opportunity
Chapter 13 - Labor and the End of Permanent jobs
Chapter 14 – The Fiscal Robbery
Chapter 15 – Bank Lending
Chapter 16 – The art of Negotiating

Conclusion

About the Author

The Basics of Financial Education

The Basics of Financial Education

Introduction

Financial education is an extensive project, especially when understood as I do: "the discipline that encompasses all those activities related to money and its consequences." Since you also use money and carry out your activities directly connected to it, you cannot ignore this discipline, and I say this in your interest. Having or not having certain knowledge and insights can determine whether your financial destiny takes one path or another. Those who don't know these subjects often make wrong choices or are forced to rely on others. In my opinion, financial education should be taught and disseminated from elementary school. However, this is not the case even at the university level. We will discuss this later. One thing is indisputable: In this society, we cannot do without money, which regulates and influences all our activities.

Four years later, in 2023, I felt it appropriate to update this book in light of recent developments, updating its content and expanding it with new chapters. We often realize how quickly time passes when we reread a book. Innovation moves fast in the financial and economic field; we must constantly update ourselves, but we must also have the basics to do so correctly. The digital age acts as a multiplier on all processes, resulting in two effects:

The Basics of Financial Education

On the one hand, innovation continues to change and improve every product, service, and content.

On the other hand, everything quickly becomes outdated, dated, and obsolete; And then there are the countless new crises of recent times: Pandemics, microchip crises, energy crises, war, inflation, drought, international destabilization, and let's hope no more are added. However, one thing remains extremely relevant and becomes more so every day: financial education. Without it, you will fall behind. I began spreading financial education (we will see the differences between financial education and financial literacy) a few years ago when we were few. Even now, there are very few "practical" disseminators of this discipline, and not everyone covers it 360 degrees. Financial education and financial literacy are two terms often used synonymously but have different meanings for me. The former includes the latter, at least according to the current understanding of financial education, a discipline more focused on the theoretical aspect of financial activities than on practice. It is seen with an academic, school-like conception. Just look at who teaches it: professors, journalists, public employees, but not entrepreneurs! For me, as long as an activity involves money, it falls within the scope of financial education. So, it is much broader than one might think.

The Basics of Financial Education

Financial education = practical approach to all activities related to money. Financial literacy = school/academic level theoretical approach to economic and financial subjects.

The first is a practical discipline and is the prerogative of those who have worked or are working as entrepreneurs or professionals in the world of business. The second is theoretical and academic and is taught by teachers or educators.

At this point, note that there is a profound difference between theory and practice. But, aside from these differentiations (as everyone thinks what they want), I believe that to talk about financial education: you must have an operational approach. You must have practiced those activities or known them directly. And not just superficially, let alone exclusively in books. Do you know how to learn all those disciplines related to financial education? In two ways: by doing business (and therefore the entrepreneur) or by working closely with businesses (for example, in banks). Yes, precisely by working in a bank where, by playing a role of trust with companies, entrepreneurs, and professionals, you can have direct and privileged access to all types of information and processes. In certain roles in a bank, you can access all information without any limits, examine and interpret it in depth, and gather it directly from the interested parties. Entrepreneurs, scientists, professionals, wealthy individuals, rich people, speculators, property owners, private and professional investors, and experts in everything open their most secret doors in the bank's rooms.

Don't believe me?

Throughout the book, I will recount various episodes to support what I claim. Also, because in my life, I have precisely done this most of the time: learning from others. All the disciplines that make up financial education are essential for us, as they provide us with the ability to understand events and manage them. They then allow us to implement in life and work those teachings that others charge as consultancy (and then issue an invoice). That's why it's good to be self-sufficient, to understand and interpret what's happening around us and what others are offering us in the form of services and consultancy.

This is crucial for taking care of your affairs, managing your family, ensuring an independent future without dependencies. For example, knowing how money works and moves is vital for each of us who have aspirations for growth. Understanding how interest rates, inflation, and currency work, reflecting on the contexts in which we are immersed and influenced, interpreting, and exploiting them, can be essential to not being caught off guard by events. Later, everyone can delve deeper into their preferred sector, and this book provides many starting points for reflection.

This is the goal: to interest the reader in exploring further in other venues the topics that suit them. In the book, you will also find some considerations on general, economic, and historical issues, which I hope will help you reflect on some themes that we sometimes fail to perceive accurately. Important themes that directly concern our future. Themes that deserve great attention and reflection, but nobody talks to us about them in the right way.

The need to inform others disinterestedly is absent in our society. Nobody is interested in informing citizens about certain topics. On the other hand, a financially educated people are not easily manipulated and managed, as governments and international lobbies want.

They make the deals, why should they leave them to us?

The Basics of Financial Education

Chapter 1

Reading and interpreting events to our advantage

The first edition of this book, originally titled "Financial Education Basics 1," was published in the year of Donald Trump's election: a highly resonant political and media event, which we used as a practical example to explain the value of financial education and the great service it provided us at that time. Although several years have passed and there is a new president in the United States, I want to revisit it, just to grasp its significance.

Trump Case

During the American election phase, polls, media, and practically all authoritative figures took Hillary Clinton's victory for granted. However, some careful observers and experts in the financial world, sensitive to signals that not everyone captured, read the opposite result; and they informed us in confidence. Basically, about 36 hours before the election, we were informed by some analysts, with whom we work, that: although Trump was still trailing in the official polls, some basic signals were unequivocally read in his favour.

In Ohio, considered the key state and the indicator for the winner in a presidential election, Trump emerged victorious. In fact, more than Clinton, he represented the people's desire for change and had spoken more clearly and directly. Private interviews with citizens showed that the protest vote was all for Trump. But above all, what convinced us of the expectation of a hypothetical victory by Trump, was a key piece of news of "office gossip ": the American financier Warren Buffet had disinvested billions of dollars from his financial assets to be liquid and ready to invest in a volatile market. And Warren Buffet, one of the richest men in the world, is rarely wrong: he had probably used his first-rate sources to make up his mind and move all that capital. An eventual victory by Trump would surely have resulted, according to all the analysts (and this time they were right), in the following consequences: the depreciation of the dollar (which it did initially: -10% but then rose again), the collapse of the Mexican currency (since Trump had promised to raise a wall with Mexico), the rise in the price of gold and oil (commodities that strengthen in times of uncertainty) and descent of the American stock market indexes in the immediate post-election due to the general confusion. Of course, more or less the opposite would have happened if Clinton had been elected, as she was the expression of the

The Basics of Financial Education

stability of government lobbies. So, with a little courage, and not by direct merit, I followed the right information sources, I invested in those six assets - thank you Warren Buffet, thank you Trump! - I hit a good result.

What happened then, in what I just told you?

Simply, the news and information that was available to all was interpreted correctly by only a few (those with proper vision and experience). So, events and information can hide great opportunities, when read correctly.

Can we therefore say that the big deals are made by going against the tide?

In this case, and in many other cases, yes. Later we will find out how and why financiers and professional investors are always in contrast, investing when the market goes down and selling when the market rises.

In the case of the US election the people were as unpredictable as the British with Brexit. I had read some of Trump's books in the past and knew his philosophy well and, regardless of the assessment that can be made about his character, he wrote interesting things about real estate and motivation. But I would have never thought he would become president of the United States of America, and that this would bring so much euphoria to the markets.

So enough with this topic, I want to explain why I started this path of financial education disclosure.

Sharing with others what you know and what you have learned through your experience and your mistakes, should be the mission of every human being.

Instead, everyone only thinks of himself, and, for fear of being surpassed by others, hides what he has learned. He is silent about any valuable information or communicates so it is only partially understood, and so on. It is the culture in which we were brought up and in which we grew up: a school where we may not give someone the answer or make a mistake, otherwise we risk being punished.

In this context and type of learning, you are encouraged to not help your classmates. It is the era of sanctions, errors and hostility between people. This exists between colleagues, families, communities, nations and at all levels. "Homo homini lupus" ("Dog eat dog") is the frequent way of operating in modern society. The current economic crisis, which began in 2007/2008 and is one of many, but perhaps the most incisive and dramatic ever, is leading many people to poverty and despair after 10 years for various reasons: lack of disposable income, work, ideals and optimism towards the future. Governments all have an interest in keeping the people in a state of general ignorance so they can tax, squander and print money at will. And the people, that is all of us, do somersaults to survive decently and to support their families or even start one, if we ever succeed in this general depression. He who has the knowledge and information does not disclose it and, in fact, preserves it jealously. That is why, having reached a certain age and a wide experience in the world of banking and business, I chose to begin publishing a series of books to spread those principles that fall under the definition of instruction or financial education that no one teaches us and never will teach us ...later we will find out why.

My goal is to urge people to study and to invest in knowledge that can change or improve their lives and maybe show them the way to achieve success. Finding your own way or changing it mid-race is not easy. Everything has been different for some years now: the world has been distorted by the web; our certainties at work have collapsed; and what we are learning is continuously changing direction. Everything is going faster and faster. You have to think differently, adapt to changes quickly, be dynamic and versatile in order to seize new opportunities. But this new world, I'm sorry to say, is not for everyone. And definitely not for those who remain anchored to the past.

The Basics of Financial Education

Chapter 2

Financial Education

What is meant by "financial education"? There are many interpretations and definitions that are given to this term. For me, financial education, a concept with a very vast extension, encompasses all those activities -- whatever their nature and to whatever discipline they belong - that have a relationship with money and what it brings. Everyone says money does not bring happiness. But can you live without money? Whether it is used to support yourself, to be invested or accumulated, we all need money and then some. It is essential for everyone. And it is the medium that allows us to satisfy any need, primary or secondary.

What prompted me to publish this book on the subject was the desire to disclose to the public the roots of financial education, which are at the basis of their daily life when talking about work, business, future prospects and so on. The idea came also from the unease that I have always felt when I have seen that every concept is complicated and made difficult and incomprehensible by the media. During my professional activities at well-known banking institutions, I

The Basics of Financial Education

have often found myself observing how much ignorance there is among people on these topics. Try to take a test. Open a newspaper, a daily newspaper and, with the utmost honesty, put a red circle around all those topics that you do not fully understand. Do the same with an economic or financial newspaper. In this way, you can easily see which topics are more understandable to you and which instead you know less about. I bet that in the financial newspaper the rate of incomprehension will be higher. And, believe me, in my experience at work I have been confronted by established professionals belonging to various categories (lawyers, accountants, notaries, university professors, bankers, business managers): whatever their sector of origin, in most cases, I realized that their financial literacy rate was indeed insufficient and incomplete.

Not to mention the average citizen! But then again, all this is the logical consequence of the absence of education in concepts of finance in primary and secondary school. I think now one thing is clear: the only one who can give you a correct financial education is you. Forget turning to your accountant or your financial consultant for help. Only you can instruct yourself in the best and most relevant way to suit your qualities. How can you succeed, how can you aspire to become an entrepreneur or simply to secure a prosperous life if you do not know the basics and fundamental mechanisms of the system? Do you think the big businessmen, financiers, those who fought for their success, do not know these notions, having learned them the hard way or from someone else? Being able to talk about any subject without being "fooled", believe me, is crucial in today's society. Of course, you cannot know everything or study everything, but a basic literacy, with the following insights, is more necessary than ever.

Here's a trivial example, taken from everyday life: marriage. When we are about to get married, and we are caught in the turbines of falling in love, are we aware of the legal and economic effects we will encounter? Or do we think the path is all "hunky-dory"? While the emotional and sentimental aspects of marriage may fade, the financial and economic aspects will bind us for life. Let's examine with a rational mind the statistics of marriages. In Northern Europe we are touching peaks of 70% of marriages failing. This is not the case in Southern Europe where sometimes no one separates officially, because the pair continues to live together for economic convenience. Surely everyone thinks "it won't happen to me, I will be in the other part of the statistics, the one of happy marriages". We hope so. But given the number of failures one must think it over carefully, before committing formally. The legal ties and costs arising from the marriage are binding and they may penalize you for life. In some countries, where the law is too rigid, the other party may advance claims

The Basics of Financial Education

even after the divorce! Even knowing all of this is financial education!

Without financial education, I have always tried to understand the meaning of things on my own. That's why I've always been a great devourer of books, mostly American, on every topic that was relevant to my training. Books on business, marketing, psychology, NLP, finance and so on, believing that this knowledge constitutes the foundation that every person should have. Financial education is not even found where one would imagine in banks, economic ministries, in financial or production companies or in professional offices. This discipline is absent in our culture and the only way to learn it is through the reading of specific texts or direct apprenticeship. However, experience practiced in the field is expensive and not everyone can afford to acquire it. It takes time and money. So the easiest and cheapest way is to follow the advice and the valuable experience of others. This is exactly what that we are going to do.

A self-study course on financial education goes through several steps: investment, risk, sometimes mistakes (who has never been wrong?), to then move on to the next level of awareness. In this path, therefore, errors are equivalent to inevitable step learning. No point of your growth is lost, everything becomes "capital" to learn from, and understanding this is crucial when you are relating to a "thing"

The Basics of Financial Education

as hard to handle as money. Dealing with money is challenging. And where does it take you? Simply to being fully responsible for your behaviour in economic and financial fields, but not only. It's important to take control of your funds (made of goods or simply of knowledge), your income and, above all, your potential and, therefore, your future. And if you are so lucky to have your own established wealth, not to let it get taken away. Or maybe to make it more productive.

Financial education is also necessary so that we can understand. Yes, but what? What the economists, politicians, or even simply, reporters say when they are talking about economy, finance, current affairs, without any clarity and using complicated language. Often, in these contexts, the concepts are complicated to the extreme and thus perceived by most people as unattainable, therefore ignored and neglected. It is as if they were saying: "Leave us to deal with your economic and financial issues, you are not capable.". And in fact, we can see the results! We are constantly robbed of our wealth and labour through fiscal robbery and the political illusion of a better future, which instead keeps getting worse ...

The language should be accessible to all, and each topic explained with examples and easy words. But now it is clear: there is the will to make it comprehensible only to a chosen few, definitely not to us commoners. Still, it's never too late

The Basics of Financial Education

to learn! These materials are not only exciting, but they open our minds to the future. At least this was the case for me. No matter what your starting point is, what counts is intelligence, insight, perseverance and the willingness to learn. In my vision, understanding what the real value of money is, the importance of the money supply mechanisms, and having a clear view of the globalization of economic scenarios is essential. If I do not understand how the world economy turns, then I'm like a little mouse in a big gear. There is no easy way to success. There is no easy way to wealth. They are both achieved through a lot of work done first on oneself and then on the outside world. You go through personal improvement, trying to highlight your strengths and your qualities to get to know the main topics that constitute financial education. Then each person becomes self-determining based on his own abilities, character, his passions and life context. In the business world there is only room for those who work hard, are willing to make sacrifices and improve themselves.

In any case ... everyone talks and writes about these topics, both in dozens of books and on the web! But between thinking you know how to do something, having actually done it and wanting to teach others, there is a huge difference. Also, in order to teach, you have to demonstrate that you have indeed achieved results in the field of cash and investments, not just that you shave read a few books and suddenly become

The Basics of Financial Education

a communicator. My work consists of financial training made up of many pieces, many ideas and suggestions that everyone will have to adapt to himself and to his own capabilities. After that, we hope, we will be successful. But success is not just "become a millionaire" as they state on many high-sounding slogans. Success is articulated on many different levels, and everyone can aspire to reach it. It depends on where we start. For someone who is unemployed, success can be constituted by creating a business that will bring an income. The disgruntled employee may begin to understand and navigate in the world outside his company. Anyone, in any situation, can aspire to something better and so on. Our aim is to help everyone to improve themselves and find personal success, according to his aspirations and his potential. This will not be easy and it will not be for everyone; it is only for those who grasp what they need to develop their financial culture.

Rule number 1: money is a commodity. Wealth is not created but moved. How? From one person to another. It happens in the stock market and takes place in everyday life. The great magnates of our time have found the idea, the enterprise, the system that makes money flow to them. Jobs, Gates, Bezos, Zuckerberg, but first Rockefeller, Soros and Buffet, have all found a way to steer rivers of money towards their portfolios. Constant, growing streams of money. Obviously, they are cases which are unique in the world and for each of them there are billions of people who are unable to establish themselves or simply to make a living. In our global society, what can the average citizen do to create or intercept a flow of money which increases his economic well-being? He can start, first of all, with the knowledge of the financial world rules. If you do not know the game and its rules you can participate, but you have little chance of success. And no one teaches you those rules: you have to learn them and search for them on your own. We will see later how.

You have to have willpower, perseverance, the desire to achieve results in overcoming failures and bad times. The stories of the men that I mentioned before (the richest in the world), as enshrined in copious biographies, testify to the fact that their successes were born from the biggest failures and the biggest disappointments, waste and skepticism of others. This has done nothing other than strengthen them temperamentally and emotionally. The best lessons are learned by making mistakes and learning from them, by acquiring the experience that allows you to not make any more mistakes in the future in similar situations.

So what should we do? We must try to insert ourselves into the money circuit, in a business, trying to keep in our pockets the money that we see passing by. Look for a cash flow and profit from it. Period. Money is the key to everything; it is the necessary path. A successful man without money, who cannot make ends meet…how successful is he? He may perhaps be

The Basics of Financial Education

in the cultural and artistic fields, but here we're talking about business. Financial success, which is power or wealth, always translates into the availability of economic resources.

But do we really know money? We should know it profoundly, in its most secret aspects if we want it to flow towards us. Money equals education on money and thus financial education. Attend seminars, courses on coaching, read books about it, try to get into the mechanisms of money. See how those who possess it behave, how they keep it safe from risks and how it multiplies through business. A person who knows money (financially educated), knows how to negotiate, and knows how to communicate, is already rich. He just needs to find a way to input his knowledge and skills into an economic flow.

First rule: do tabula rasa, in our minds, of all the commonplaces! Those we were taught in school, by family, newspapers and others in general. We need to replace our obvious and wrong beliefs with new and fruitful convictions. Let's steer clear of all the opinions of friends and family, by skeptics who dismantle everything and know everything. Tabula Rasa. Clear your mind. Now we will start to put into it some basic principles, maybe some you have never heard of or were never taught. Then let's build on that, with our critical spirit, a method and a project. It is a slow process, but it leads to the result. First analysis: your education. What type of education do you have? How did you obtain it? How can it be integrated and improved? Do you have a mentor, a coach who can help and support you in your path? If you do not, do not worry there are publications, courses on-line, business books. We must first understand the current context: where we are now and how we got here. Then we have to study other contexts of the past that will probably return since the economy works in cycles. We have to understand what gives us a result and what does not. You have to study money, real estate, business activities, national and international contexts. Then learn some principles of negotiation, communication, economics. Then we will be ready. But do we have the humility to study all of this? In this road to financial education, I assure you, we all start from a more or less basic level, and each one can emerge with respect to millions of fellow citizens. Our perception of others, with respect to this topic, is often wrong. Appearance can easily fool us and let those who know less than we do pass for someone who knows more. Have you ever wondered, for example, why some rich and successful people go to get advice from those who know less than they, and who aren't even remotely close to their wealth and their position? I often quote this phrase, which I have always appreciated: "Wall Street is the only place where the rich go in a Rolls Royce to get advice from those who go to work in the subway ... ". Because many of them, in spite of appearances, know little about money even if they possess a lot.

Chapter 3

Self-training shock

Speaking of working on yourself, let's look at some practical examples. I'll tell you about two real life experiences and two important insights. Perhaps they will seem a bit daring, but they worked wonderfully. Let's say it's a sort of self-punishing, self-training experience. I purposely put this chapter at this point in the book to reinforce the theme of self-determination, without which the path towards financial freedom is more difficult.

The bus technique.

Enter alone in a crowded bus at rush hour. Then, suddenly, begin speaking loudly to everyone, attracting their attention, as if you were at the theater. Then, when the scene is over, get off at the next stop. I remember that I was able to do this only at the third attempt. It was a task that was not at all easy to take on. Then, on the fourth I attempt, I began like so: "Hello my name is ... not my real name .... and I would like to share a poem with you that is close to my heart (it was the only one that I knew by heart). Please listen to me ... " And I began to recite out loud, but quickly, the first part of a poem that I had been forced to memorize in school, "In the shadow of cypress trees and in the urn ..." ("The Tombs" by Ugo Foscolo). A few stanzas, not too short nor too long, just long enough for everyone to listen and pay attention. After the recitation came the worst moment: I had carried out my psychological punishment and I had to get off the bus. The wait for the next bus stop (there was suddenly a lot of traffic) was a nightmare, it seemed to never arrive. From the moment the poem ended to when the bus doors opened (which seemed to last forever) I had to endure the looks, giggles, comments and the indifference of those who were around me and did not know where to look or where to hide. Once I got off the bus I felt like a lion again. I had had the courage to do an experiment that I had never thought I could do. I would not have seen those people ever again, but I had been tested on something very daring and emotionally very difficult. At that time there was a great desire to question and test oneself in difficult situations.

The cold-examination madness.

Another technique that I put into practice when I was 22 years old was even more drastic and irresponsible: the University Exam. Not just any University, the one where I was attending my undergraduate program. I'll tell you what happened, because I remember it very well and whenever I tell the story,

The Basics of Financial Education

I relive it. It was a powerful experience, but effective for my training and it took place completely by chance and not because of me. At least in the beginning.

We went as a group to see the exams of I don't know what subject in the course of Law. As a joke, some of my classmates took me to the course where a different exam was being held than the one, we had chosen to attend. An exam that I would have had to take the following year. Our student spirit pushed us to get in all kinds of trouble at the time. While we were outside of the exam classroom, my friends told me that they had signed me up for the examination a few minutes before being called in alphabetical order. Everything had been well organized and then, after a few smiles and their mocking me, I thought that the joke was over. As I was usually the initiator of these pranks against each other, this time they were doing to it me, and it irritated me a lot. I did not expect it. So, not wanting to give in, as well as wanting to challenge myself and to show my courage, I decided to tempt fate. With the recklessness that characterized me at that age, and the love for risk-taking that I had always had, I announced to my friends: "I'm going ... I'll show you that I am not afraid ... I'll do the examination, I'll challenge everyone."

I was, of course, completely unprepared and a bit crazy. I thought to myself: "I'll use it as quick, self-study course on overcoming shyness and insecurity, giving my friends a slap in the face and demonstrating the courage of a lion. " I wanted to win. It was late morning and while I was mulling this over and organizing myself mentally, the janitor called my name out loud and the classroom door was closed. I did not know what was waiting for me in there, but I decided to risk it. I went in and saw this scene: a large hall, larger than those at school, with a desk in the center. All around it were desks with no chairs and dozens, perhaps hundreds, I do not know, of students crowding around, sitting or standing listening to the exams. They were so many that I had to push and shove my way through to get to the center of the classroom to reach the professor that was examining the students. I heard my last name called again and then a second time; my legs were shaking, my blood was circulating at supersonic speed, my blood pressure had to be at full speed. Also, because I knew nothing. Tabula rasa, not even a subject of my own choosing for that exam. A less important course, but still law exam. It was not even a conversational examination where you could bluff your way through; it was a historical examination.

I went on, breathing deeply, watching the students around me out of the corner of my eyes. More than one of them on the way gave me a pat on the shoulders and wished me "good luck". David and Goliath, a non-existent preparation in front of a fountain of information: the professor. Yes, he was the head professor of an important tenure, a distinguished author of texts on the subject who, that day, without making use of assistants, had decided to test the students directly. But the assistants were all around him and instilled even more fear in the general silence. Well, I put on a smile and sat down.

"Good morning," said the professor, a man of about 55 years, very empathetic, which cordially lessened my tension. "Good morning," he said, "I see you are agitated, are you nervous?"

"Yes, pretty much" I said and started to improvise saying "I'm pretty nervous Professor because I'm afraid I don't I remember much; I studied for this exam a few months ago and then I had some personal problems so I couldn't review anything. "

"Oh, I'm sorry," he said, "let's try to test ourselves and get through the first topic ". Endless moments until he formulated the question.

"Tell me about ..." and he asked the question. Topic, alas, unknown to me, incomprehensible and mysterious. Tabula Rasa. I pretended to think for a moment, pretending to strain myself. I confess that by now I was perfectly relaxed, the anxiety was gone, the fear as well. I even became a little arrogant. I had identified myself completely with what I said, that I really was a model student who had studied the subject and was prepared, who had a good grade point average (which was true), and that for real life family problems of a personal nature, had not reviewed and therefore could not remember anything. It seemed true; I made it true in my mind.

I rolled my eyes to heaven and said: "Professor, I have a sort of amnesia, I cannot remember the subject."

He replied: "Well it can happen. Tell me about ... " and he fired off another question, which was followed by a more or less similar answer to the preceding one.

"I see that you are quite nervous!" said the professor, "you told me it's been a long time since you studied this subject, but you prepared for it in the past. Well then, to break the ice, talk about a subject that you remember, a free topic as you desire, and then we will go one from there... "

How embarrassing! I had not even studied the typical favorite topic... Maybe, who knows, I could have saved myself or I could have emerged from this with dignity: then again, I had presented myself on the spot, without even having a day to think about it. With my usual eyes raised to the ceiling and masterful intuition, for how I had recited, I said, "Thank you, Professor, you are very polite and helpful, but I think at this point in the examination, having failed the first two questions, it is not the case for me to continue. Also, because I already have a good grade point average and I would like to raise it further, so I prefer to stop up now and try again at the next session, so I can hit the books and review the subject well, hoping to get a high mark and hopefully this will happen again with you. Thanks anyway".

He nodded, shook my hand, almost feeling sorry for me! I got up and as I was walking away realized that all around me were hundreds of people watching me leave, in a deathly silence. I proudly walked to the door (again, those moments seemed endless) and left the room. Once I shut the door behind me and ended the embarrassing ordeal, I was engulfed with such a sense of power and satisfaction that I cannot describe. It was as if I had completed a memorable enterprise. I had overcome my emotions, fears, shyness, had challenged the others while standing tall and had demonstrated my courage and guts of steel to my friends. And none of them, I think, would have had the courage to do the same. In short, I came out an overall winner. I would have further gained their respect and even admiration. I had stood up for myself in front of hundreds of people who unintentionally had been used for my experiment in testing myself and my self-training!!!

I felt strong, powerful. I had been through an incredible test of courage, boldness, heroism almost, according to my then state of mind. Since at the time I was introverted and shy, this test made me stronger. I had challenged everyone and had come out a winner. Once this was done, I thought, what other challenge would I have to fear? With whom should I be afraid to speak or deal with if I had been able to speak on equal terms with a professor, fooling him and all the others, in front of hundreds of people who listened to me and with such impudence? And it is true, since then I have had no more problems dealing with anyone: I became stronger, more confident, more determined and I am still benefitting from this today. It was a drastic lesson, but a very effective one.

This is the art of negotiating. Do not fear a face-off with anybody. In my professional life I am always the one who gets sent ahead when it comes to talking or dealing with the most difficult or challenging entrepreneurs. And this has forged me even further. Would you be able to carry out the experiment as well? There are thousands of schools: for coaching, self-esteem, marketing, etc., etc. But the best school is the one that everyone can attend alone on oneself. What's the secret? Always think what I think before facing a difficult situation: in the end, how long will it last? It is a short-term misery and then there will be liberation. You just have to hold out for a few minutes, then it's over. Like when we have a shot. The needle enters: we suffer. The seconds while the liquid penetrates seem endless. Then we feel the massage and we understand that the needle has come out ... and the state of well-being and positivity returns to us.

The Basics of Financial Education

Well, this is the same thing. Developing these qualities is not difficult, it takes application, a bit of recklessness and the courage to jump since it's over soon. But after we will have great advantages. Artists, musicians, our idols also have their weaknesses and do not always manage to be as strong as they seem, so much so that many of them ruin their lives with the help of drugs and alcohol. For the experience the be effective and sink in you need to be in complete control and the cure must be the most drastic possible. And the act will be carved in your brain and be treasured there to bring out your character and strength.

I discovered after many years, after all, that this was an NLP technique and that these experiments are encoded in various procedures. But at the time I did not know. Perhaps NLP was not even known at that time...Then, perhaps on another occasion, I'll tell you some other episodes based on the experience of trial and error and other interesting situations that I have experienced. Our culture and our school don't teach this to us. They lead us to believe that it is forbidden to make a mistake. If you mess up, they give you a bad grade. While, in fact, we learn from our mistakes. When I started doing professional trading, in my leisure time of course (the evening mostly), I began to get interested in platforms, brokers, options, forex, etc. etc. and all the information useful to approach the trading industry, which is basically different from the investment banking sector that instead knew well. I

The Basics of Financial Education

was assigned, as is usually the case, a demo account with which to practice and learn the various tasks. Well, after so many years now I know myself, and I knew that I would never use the demo account. I risked real money from day one. Because I know that if I don't make a mistake in person, if I don't face failure, if I do not make mistakes, and if the impact is not dramatic with a real adrenaline rush, I do not learn. Or rather, let's say that learning is much faster and more effective when the impact is drastic.

Just like when you learn to swim if you are thrown in the water unceremoniously. I remember at first with trading I lost some money, then more, then even more, until I cancelled out the benefits of a deal that had ended a few months before. But I did not give up. Then one day, when I hit bottom, I began to rise gradually, as if I had learned the system. And it was there that I realized that I had learned the lesson and finally I could invest more money to create an account that today is quite productive when I devote some time to it. But we will get back to this at a later time.

Trading is in fact one of those activities that you can start from home, and which allows you to form capital over time (but beware! It's not easy: the risks are many and quite treacherous, the success rates are low). We hope not to have bored you with these small, but significant, personal experiences. I assure you that these few, dramatic episodes were enough to get a distinctive improvement in my ability to deal with others and to negotiate, and to overcome hesitations and fear. In this regard each of us can do better, also because each person, if he is honest with himself, knows himself better than anyone else and no coach, psychologist or mind expert can do better than anyone can do alone on himself.

The Basics of Financial Education

Chapter 4

Economy and Investment

If we try to look up the word economy and its meaning some very difficult and sometimes abstruse concepts appear. This should absolutely not be the case. What does "economy" mean? It derives from the greek "Oikonomos" which means "those who deal with family". So "economy" refers to a series of actions and behaviors that should be used to manage a household, a company, a country and so on. But is this your understanding of it? I remember that, at the university, economics was one of those subjects that fascinated me, but it felt like it was abstract and complex to understand. There was no talk of real life, of current events, and not talk of crisis. Already at the time (we're talking about the 70s) there was a crisis, as there is today. Of course, a different crisis! But no one ever mentioned it at school ... The study of traditional economic models has had its day. The economy has freed itself with globalization of the mechanisms of the past. We have to reform teaching in universities. It is what we preach with financial and economic training. The market is global, there is no longer a local economy but a transnational one. Our thinking must branch out from domestic logistics and project itself in a total universe. Today you can publish a book in the world with a simple click, you can communicate in real time with all the citizens of the planet and make economic and financial transactions in real time. In addition, there are no longer secrets that we can take from one place to bring to another: everything is already "on-line" and therefore the effort to invent, to create and innovate is much greater. This global dimension is not yet fully perceived, but we would do well to adopt it. He who is at the forefront, uses internet and social networks well is light years ahead. The old man has suddenly become obsolete, everything is changing at uncontrollable speeds.

Before today, mail reached us after a few days; today in real time. We are available 24/7 through our tablets and smartphones and, therefore, there is no more dead time. The malls are open non-stop; the typically Mediterranean habits of "take it easy" are ending. At work, in the same way, everything is quick and constantly changing. Only active and dynamic minds can adapt. Everything is accessible via the web and immediately, without waiting. Managers are always "on-line", even while on vacation and young people are constantly connected to each other and never put aside their smartphones. The boss is looking for you ... your wife is looking for you ... you have to always be available.

I do not know if it's little, but all this changes everything: work, your free time, relationships with others, aspirations.

The Basics of Financial Education

Just adapt, get in line and go. This sudden enormous speed also affects the economy, which is accustomed to having slower and weighted cycles. The digital quake has had an impact on timing, on cycles and on ways in which the economy has an impact on citizens and businesses. The latter in particular are disoriented in front of changes they have never faced before and that require structural and organizational changes. The economy works in cycles that last for limited periods of time. Speed has accelerated the duration of these economic cycles and globalization has extended them simultaneously around the Western world; the repercussions have a direct impact on countries and on citizens' lives.

Economic cycles last for limited periods of time and precisely because we are talking about cycles, we must expect, sooner or later after a crisis, a phase of expansion and economic revival. After a strong crisis the first signs are clear. So, our behavior should follow the economic cycle and even try to predict it, to try to take advantage of the opportunities of thinking in ahead. We must prepare ourselves to welcome a new phase of economic growth thinking that, in a few years, today's opportunities will no longer be available.

The stock market is a fantastic example of cyclicality. If we take a look, quite simply, at the market graphs now easily available on the internet, from the 1900s to today we will see a graph made up of ups and downs. We see that economic crises are represented by downward peaks, then there are new upward cycles and then new crises. This graph reflects, broadly speaking, the performance of the economy since the stock market is the representation of the economic performance of listed companies. This also happens in real estate where there are ups and downs. The fact of being in a "low" phase only gives us the certainty that soon (although the timing is uncertain) there will be a cycle upwards. And vice-versa. That's why experts, financiers and real estate developers do not care about the collapses. They know they must simply take adequate precautions and that you can earn in each phase, upward or downward. Indeed, the more the fluctuation is high and volatile the more the market is enhanced and there are revenue opportunities. But beware! This is what the experts do. Instead, non-experts, ordinary people, savers, are intimidated by any drop, as they are also the victims of what the newspapers say, which often scare people with sensationalistic headlines.

So what does the average saver do? When there is a slump he sells (and loses) and when there is a rise, enticed by earning, he buys (which is risky because he is buying at already raised prices). Instead, what does the professional investor do? When there is a collapse: he buys. When here is an rise, he sells. He always makes money. The "cattle park"-- this is the unflattering expression with which citizens, savers and non-professionals are defined --always or almost always loses. And others earn the money that they lose, as we said - remember? - that wealth is not created but moved. Every fall brings money to the pockets of market professionals, money which comes out of the pockets of the poor belonging to the "cattle park". Switching from the "cattle park" to the bullpen of professional investors, or simply the experts, is only a matter of knowledge and instruction on the subject.

This rule, which we will borrow from Benjamin Graham, and which is, according to me, already worth gold in his simplicity, leads us to suggest that:

1) If we see euphoria in the markets, with headlines praising earnings, invitations to invest, rosy words about the future, then we do nothing, let us pause to reflect and analyze data. We should stay out of the market and wait.

2) When conversely, we hear praises of market crashes, general crises, crisis of this or that sector, it is time to start think about investing, of getting into the market (of course after analyzing data and opportunities).

The art of investing rationally was taught and disseminated around 1930 by one of the greatest scholars of markets and investment strategies, "our own" Benjamin Graham, who was also the professor and teacher of the greatest contemporary investor, Warren Buffet. A Finance professor at Columbia

The Basics of Financial Education

University of New York, one of the most prestigious American universities, Graham, had already identified at that time the formula of a careful and secure investment of that time: the so-called "value investing". This concept triggered a new school of thought: "When in Doubt, Stay Out". This formula consists of investing based on the fundamentals of a company, its real value, at a reasonable price, taking into consideration some basic principles.

To give you a practical example, I could mention the largest current company for turnover and worth: Apple. According to the principles of Graham today It should not be bought because it has already expressed its full (or almost maximum) price level. It may still go up but that is not certain to happen; it could actually easily fail to maintain a competitively difficult leadership record. One should have bought in years ago, when analyzing the sales data, projects and management, it would have been easy for an analyst to understand that the company was going to grow. Of course, if you had purchased at the "garage days" of Jobs and Wozniak…

It's better to invest in an unknown company that has concrete prospects for growth, rather than a well-known company that has already produced a lot from the point of view of its worth, we can simplify it like that. A serious investment focuses on the growth of the business in the future, and it develops over time. The greatest work of Graham, considered the bible of investors, is "The Intelligent Investor". This book has been called by Warren Buffet "the best book on investments ever written" and he adds "I read this book almost 60 years ago, and there I learned everything I needed." The approach of Graham to equity investment is absolutely rational and logical and is the opposite of the approach by taken the majority of investors, which is essentially emotional. This methodology has made Warren Buffet, the student who applied it, a billionaire among the richest in the world. Graham said: "The true investor in common stock does not need a large amount of brain and knowledge, but rather uncommon personal qualities."

Graham continues: "The economic conditions may change, companies and stocks may change, the financial institutions and the legal conditions may change, but human nature remains essentially the same. So the hardest and most important part of a good investment depends on the temperament and the attitude of the investor." Basically, to simplify, Professor Graham argued that investing in markets must be kept separate from an emotional approach. And that every investment is not given by the price or listing, but by the substance that is in that company. There are many examples we could make, but every investment should keep into account good companies which have possibly not yet exploded on the market, which have credible ideas and plans for the future and have investment potential in markets where they can establish and consolidate themselves, and especially that can be purchased at a reasonable price. Every stock market investment is long term. Otherwise, we are talking about trading, which is something else and bets on volatility and fluctuations of securities in the short term. Buy a diversified portfolio of companies, which you believe in, and wait for the right time, do not get carried by price, euphoria or fear, or from the headlines. This is what Graham meant.

As for the real estate sector, where I always recommend to people to invest, the same general rules explained before also apply, although more diluted over time. In fact, the variations in the real estate market are slow and last years, while the stock market is fast, almost immediate. So in real estate you have more time to meditate, analyze, think and negotiate prices. Even the matters in equity investment, as indeed those in real estate investments, will be addressed in subsequent publications where we can go more in-depth. We will close the topic of markets and equities here for now. The basic financial education is made up of lots of other factors and encompasses many other aspects, perhaps closer to the citizen. Let's move on.

Chapter 5

Educational Context

A few months ago, I was exchanging views with a student who had just graduated and was about to leave to attend a prestigious master's program in the footsteps of some of his university mates with whom he had kept in touch. From their conversations, the told the young man, emerged a sense of disappointment that after primary and secondary school, a high school diploma, a degree and a prestigious master's degree, brilliant young minds, fresh from their studies and quite receptive, were transforming into the unemployed. They went from a career of being students to being unemployed with no career, a burden to society and their family of origin. And the question he asked me, knowing of my work and my position, was: "Can you tell me what's the use of school if it does not guarantee you a profession or a job? What's the use of studying hard for almost twenty years continuously, with hard work and making all kinds of sacrifices, to end up being unemployed and having to invent yourself a future? Or maybe end up working as a waiter to support yourself?" Many of his friends with a master's degree had in fact gone to London to work as waiters as they tried to come up with some ideas about their future.

The Basics of Financial Education

Well, I too have studied a lot and for many years: a bachelor's degree, specializations, contests, training schools, to end up doing nothing connected to my studies. But times were different, and it was still possible to work on more fronts and find a job with a little knowledge, luck and application. There was less competition than there is today.

My answer to that young man was: "School, college, masters, and so on, are used exclusively by each of us to open our minds, to exercise it, to build a general culture that will be useful, but will not guarantee that we find a job. And they are not necessary to teach us how to face life and earn money. A dentist just out of university knows how to put his hands in the mouths of patients just as much as I do. He has to learn with practice. So does the doctor. So does the lawyer. They have created a layer of notions which, when put together with experience, will turn them into a good doctor or a good lawyer. But none of them knows anything about money, about how you earn or save it or how to make it multiply.

"So," I said to the young man, "when you get your master's degree call me and I will suggest how to start a path, your financial training, without which you will lose more precious time. You might find a job, elbowing your way through the job market, but it would probably not be what you want. We have millions of unmotivated and dissatisfied employees, with a barely sufficient income, but are earning even less than

The Basics of Financial Education

before and with fewer guarantees, without even the certainty of retirement. Even those who earn well, but this is always subject to the will of another, sooner or later feel the urge to escape and to change. The era of the permanent position is over... The school system produces financial illiterates. People who do not even know where to start. In fifteen years of studies a few months of intense financial education would suffice to allow everyone to move more easily into society and have a more precise idea about their future. But the state, politics and people that impose educational programs have no interest in this happening. They make the deals; they do not want competitors and especially they do not want "thinking beings" that they may become hazardous to their hold on power. This happens all over the world. The schools award the "nerds" and instead discourages creative students who have new and different ideas. It always has been this way. Those who are not aligned with the will of the professors, who often are not up to the educational task, are marginalized. But probably that student who is a bit "alternative", who does not get good grades, will be one in life who has more to say than the model student. The most capable people in life were not model students.

This old school mentality has to change, because in society these concepts have already changed. This is old news in the workplace and companies are using more and more assertive and non-directive methods. They reward initiative and innovation. The dress code itself has changed from formal to casual. The person with something new to say is listened to more and not opposed. We are seeking to overcome old patterns made of rigid hierarchies not based on merit. Then again, the organization of corporate structures derives from military systems and ecclesiastical organizations which worked as long as the world communicated slowly and with traditional systems. As long as it was possible to keep everything circumscribed and under control. Let's take a look at politics. With the spread of instant communication dictatorships are in large part crumbling (look at North Africa and the Middle East) and rigid corporate hierarchies have softened. Everything is more liquid and less rigid. Everyone communicates and speaks in real time, making it impossible to remain isolated. The protest movements are running rampant in the world and even politics seems to have the desire to change. Finally. Well in this general framework of change why don't schools and universities route us towards work and allow the most original and innovative minds t emerge? The world is already ahead; the school has lagged behind....

We continue to study archaic subjects, though not less important, such as Latin, Greek, philosophy, geometry, physics, chemistry, history, geography, art, and I've forgotten many others. These subjects give us an important cultural stratum, they broaden your mind, but in practical terms, do

The Basics of Financial Education

not help us in life and work. They should be accompanied by subjects that contain teachings on money, banking, finance, business and communication, which for now are not found basic school and university programs. Maybe there are in some specialized programs, but by then it is too late...these are subjects which should be taught to young people: they must be part of basic educational training. There is no great interest on the part of those who create the school curriculum (Governments and politicians, influenced by International Lobbies) to educate the population. We see projects of school and university reform, which are always the same old reheated soup. They do not want true reform to be implemented.

The Basics of Financial Education

Chapter 6

Informational Context

Many times, in my life I have felt entangled, unable to reason broadly, unable to let my thoughts breathe, to let my mind explore territories made of passions, aspirations, desires and dreams. And, very often, I have come out of that state of cerebral restraint, made of routines and daily neuroses, by reading a book or imagining and dreaming with open eyes. Reading a book, a text, an article, a thought, lets our minds breathe. It makes us think and project forward. Reading means just that. Writing instead means spreading information, putting our experiences and knowledge to the service of others, exposing them to the critical spirit of our neighbor. In every man or woman, there is something to say, there is something to communicate to others, the result of an experience or a simple intuition or the need to express oneself. And to be effective all you need is inspire in the other a reflection, a thought, or make an idea or change take place. Then it will have served a noble purpose. At least for me it has often been so.

The Basics of Financial Education

Have you ever tried to write a book? Maybe you have had the idea, as happened to me several times. So much effort in trying to be clear, to find interesting insights. The writers in the world are millions and millions but only a few are read and very few succeed. Only a few have made history with their works. Have you ever wondered how many books there are in libraries (and always new and different)? And how many millions of books have disappeared? Writing is one of many innate abilities in humans, an expression of one's inner self which he exposes towards others. Also because basically, you can write stories, poems, essays, novels, treaties, etc., etc. Writing is a way of communicating. The great religions have been handed down through and the great works of literature have given us infinite emotions. Reading a book in this technological age, which more and more digital and fast, has an ancient but irreplaceable feeling.

The subject that we are treating can have only three sources of learning: publications, teaching by a coach or direct experience. Information is missing from this role call. Before we talk about our vision of the world of information, I want to tell you exactly what I think of our living situation, of our real condition of evolved living beings, civilized and globalized, but also indoctrinated and influenced. In actions and in thought. I do not know how many of you know Orwell's "1984" (which, moreover, was used with great insight by Steve Jobs in a well-known Apple advertising

The Basics of Financial Education

campaign) in which the great brother (the Party) watched over the lives of citizens and at all times and they could not even think of deviations from it. Our condition in the Western world, however, is to live in freedom. But is this true? Are we sure? In addition to overt coercion, there is also subliminal and devious influence, that creeps into our brains without us even noticing. The majority of citizens, with an average education, is easily influenced and psychologically manipulate. In my opinion, to induce "people" to stop thinking and in this way be less problematic, there has been an increase in the speed and bustle in work and your everyday life. So really don't have the time to think about anything except your workday and bringing home your salary.

If we read Noam Chomsky, the great thinker of our century, we have a clear model of what happens in our information society. He who controls or manipulates the information, through the spread or omission of news, controls the views of citizens and can govern undisturbed. The subliminal power of the media is devastating. Ever wonder why when there is a coup, the first to deal with it is the headquarters of the television networks? Even before government offices?

The TV news: the more the news tells us of reports of crime, blood and grim scandals, the more they want to impress us as they are silent about fundamental news on politics or opinions. They keep quiet about a negative period of adverse political events and instead feed us sensational news: rapes, teachers who hit children, old people who are abused in care homes. Events and sports news are exalted beyond their actual value in the news. These stories and these events happen every day, but they are never discussed. They are spoken of only when needed; but it's not that when the focus is shifted elsewhere these events do not continue to happen. They are pulled out when the object is to dilute, divert and influence the public. The way I see it the news should report the news aseptically. Period. It is reasonable that there are some journalistic insights, but they should just give the news and only the news. Then the audience can formulate an idea and develop his critical sense. The commentators should be put in opposition to voice different factions, but the news should be given as it is in reality.

Try, instead, to flip through the news shows. Does anyone act like this? The same goes for newspapers and their headlines that enhance or suppress the topics in favour of or opposed to its editorial direction. It is almost always political. Are there independent publishers? I am not aware of any independent publishers who control the mass media. Those in power also influence the media to strengthen their impact on the population. That said, I hope I have provoked some reflection taking into account that: "He who reads the newspapers is not informed, he is influenced ..."

The Basics of Financial Education

I want to briefly dwell on the thought of the great 87-year-old philosopher I've mentioned before, whom I invite you to read if you can: Noam Chomsky. He offers a scientific representation of the media and information that I fully share, and I could not express better. Here I will share several passages. Chomsky argues that, in essence, the media that provides information is a kind of company that sells a product: ratings, which is sells to advertising companies for a profit. The higher the ratings of the news shows, which are then filled with segments that raise the ratings at that time, the more the advertisers pay to place their commercials before and after the news shows.

The image that the media wants to give the world is the one that is interests those who have to sell advertising: the multinationals and politicians. The managers, directors and editorialists who create information have direct links and interchange roles with politics (the journalist takes on a political role and, conversely, the politician writes a book or becomes a journalist, and they collaborate together). Europe, the US and the western world, are full of such examples of blending politics, journalism and information. All share careers and do business together, release books, influence public opinion or steer it to a given thought. So far nothing new. Except politics and governments, which have access to inside information and offer exclusive information and "tip-offs" to organs of press they consider "friends", demanding in return submission and influence on the editorial front. Up to the point of piloting or manufacturing news or keep other news in a secondary position at certain times or historical periods. One can also use the tools of slander or of piloted defamation. And we see this in newspapers quite often.

The mass media is made up of television, but also editorial newspapers, schools, universities, academic studies and so on. This articulated system produces the so-called "propaganda" that addresses about 20% of the educated population, at a high level, which plays a role in the decision-making mechanism. They are the ones who may, through their influence, define the guidelines and implementation of political action. Then there is the remaining approximately 80% of the population, the one which works and has no time, the one that suffers the decisions, the one which, for the most part, the media addresses. This system acts by influencing and distracting, directing opinions so they do not give discomfort to the traditional political class, the one that holds the power. It puts a "state" veil in front of the events of the world, hiding the true reality which if it were instead known by all in its entirety, would lead to the emergence of movements or the desire to change or the exercise of thought. And it is precisely by opposing this phenomenon today that new opposing movements are emerging, and citizens are voting in an unexpected way. We saw this with Trump, with Brexit and with some European referendums.

The Basics of Financial Education

The aim is to create a state of passivity, or rather, of non-political activities. It is not necessary to take an interest in what happens in the world. Actually, it is not desirable: knowing the true reality brings to mind the desire to change it. So the ruling elites maneuver information and news so very subtly and intelligently by filtering or manipulating them with the sole purpose of maintaining power and keeping the population in "a state of indecision". This process, at first premeditated, is now consolidated and continues on its own. Maybe even those who implement it do not even think of it anymore and they act according to a proven and consolidated mechanism that has been handed down, and so on. "The masses must in some way be distracted. They can be fed emotionally powerful illusions. The main directive is, however, to exclude them: let them do insignificant things, let them scream for a football team or have fun with a soap opera. What one needs to do is create a suitable system in which each individual remains glued to the cathode ray tube.

A well-known principle of totalitarian cultures is the desire to isolate individuals: it is extremely important to keep them separate. When the majority is together it may come up with some strange ideas. If you keep individuals isolated, it is not interesting if they think and what they think. So, we have to keep people isolated, and in our society that means keeping them glued to the television or to the internet in their spare time from work. A perfect strategy. You are completely passive and pay attention to things that are completely insignificant and have no effect. You're obedient. You're a consumer. You buy junk which you don't need. And you don't bother anyone. The goal, experts say, is to "control the minds of people who otherwise would represent the biggest danger large multinationals could face." Chomsky's is a fascinating thought, completely sharable: just look at our reality. Let's develop our own critical thinking; let's distrust other people's interpretations. Let's seek out direct sources of information. Only in this way can information--the true wealth in circulation, available at no charge in every possible form--may be freely filtered by our minds, through our beliefs and our principles.

Human beings are influenced, directly or indirectly, in many ways. We are constantly exposed to plagiarism of every kind without realizing it. In a society governed by the polls, where the only thing that matters is consent, where surveys influence the same surveys and the undecided go where the masse leads them, there can be no objectivity. To be objective is very difficult and requires a great inner balance and a strong personality, with a habit of critical thinking. That not all citizens possess. Because there is no time to think, read or reflect: we must work for a living and everything is always faster, exasperated and leaves no space for anything. By focusing on these aspects, I sincerely hope to have aroused in you some doubts and some serious meditating.

Chapter 7

Economic Context

We live in change. We are in the midst of a digital revolution. In the past the industrial revolution changed our lives, as did the technological revolution, but the digital one is more complex and articulated and most of all is unpredictable and moves at unexpected speeds. And like the others is irreversible.

The web has shaken up every principle of entrepreneurship and economics startling the most influential economists and opinion-leaders, who, being of another generation, are anchored to the past. Many of us are likely to become obsolete, in life and in work. Personally, I try to adapt every action and every project affecting the future to this new reality. If we don't subvert our principles and beliefs to a global vision, no longer sector-specific or at a local level, we will not make sense of this. But what can be done? How should we reason? How should we make plans? I see young people, the millenials and adolescents, enter with increasingly incisiveness in the present, and I see how they manage to understand everything much more effectively. And how they develop new methods of communication and new modes to interact. Every day there are huge strides forward. But do we realize it?

I believe that many are not fully aware of this, and they see themselves, the companies they possess and the families they drive, fall back more and more. Then you find yourself suddenly cut off. This happens for many commercial activities and many shops you see in the streets; they have not figured out where the world is heading. The e-commerce is advancing in double figures and the items you can buy through it are the same that we find in the stores, whose sales are gradually decreasing from day to day...until the businesses close. Look around you, examine the area where you live. How many historic shops have closed? How many new shops have opened in their places and then likewise have closed or are in the process of doing so? They didn't understand...In the banks we analyze the turnover and behaviour of companies: we perceive these phenomena before they happen. The digital companies are exploding whereas traditional businesses are languishing.

The one market that appears to be resisting on the streets is the food business. A clothing store or other commodity closes (maybe historic) and it place opens a bar, a fast-food restaurant, a bistro... It is the new fashion. This is because you cannot sell food "online": you have to eat and you have to be physically present but...this is an important indicator. Competition in this sector has become exasperated and despite all these new businesses continue to open. Streets once famous for their shops now seem to be streets for food! Too bad that, while supply increases dramatically, the demand has remained stable. The customers have remained the same, and they distribute themselves among merchants reducing the profit margins for all. How many of you have observed this phenomenon as well? Those who open a shop on the street today risk a lot. Especially if it sells items that you can also find on the web, on Amazon, on e-commerce websites and so on. On the internet payments are easy and fast. Deliveries are practically within 24 hours, shipping costs do not affect the price, no one answers we "do not have it", "I've run out, I have to order it" ... etc. etc… We purchase from the couch at home or from our smartphones given all these benefits it is obvious that such a system will take over! Just get over your initial mistrust, buy your first item and then you're hooked... But how can a shopkeeper with a traditional mindset start selling on the web? He only knows how to be a shopkeeper and tries again and again to stand out in the market, but the selection is ruthless...the ending goes without saying.

I do not know if what we are saying is clear or seems futuristic, but we are with both feet in this process. How long it will take depends on the situation, the town, the people; but it is now irreversible. And this, in our financial education route, we cannot ignore. So, dear readers, step into the web world, study it, take an interest, understand it and overcome your reticence. Otherwise, it will be painful. Companies are in the same conditions as the general public: only some are understanding and are changing, or at least are trying to do so, but it's hard. If the field is not attractive, it will be a problem to change course. I see this also in my industry, with banks. A few are gearing up to survive. Few are driven by people who have understood. In fact, what it is going on? Failures and bailouts are the order of the day...but eventually only the strongest species will survive, one that evolves.

The symbol of this is an image that dates back to 2008, when the economic crisis began: two years later, in 2010, Christie's Auction House offered the "Lehman Brothers" sign which had become a simple heirloom. That trademark, which represented one of the most powerful and respected banks in the world, which with its economic strength could bring down any multinational, was now a relic to be displayed!

History

Let's analyze our economic and financial situation using as broad a perspective as possible. Over the centuries companies have evolved from simple social organizations to increasingly complex structures. Passing through the social, industrial, computer and digital revolutions, our society has become so complex and contaminated by visible and invisible powers, it cannot be easily understood for what it represents. Countries, politics, economics and, above all, finance, are driven by so-called powers or groups of international power, which govern our lives with the sole purpose that counts in the capitalist era: profit and enrichment. Politics, marketing, communication: everything is aimed at profit for a few. And if there are errors, the bill is paid for by the citizens. And they must be paid. Immediately and without question.

The citizen is an ant inserted into a mechanism which is so complicated that many of us during our lifetime do not even question whether this is lawful or fair or legal. Schooling and higher education are imposed on us, as is our income and we are maneuvered through the use of manipulated information. Few, very few, they have the ability and strength to stop reflect and try to decipher these phenomena. Everything is taken for granted, our brains are tuned in and connected to a common thought. To the common necessities. The ground breakers, as were some great people in history, those who created the break with traditional models, no longer see able to be able to emerge today as they are suffocated by the mechanisms. Here history is our teacher. Man has not changed his attitude: he is still greedy, aggressive, tending to be arrogant towards the weak. There have always been wars, continuously and in all parts of the world. Two peoples became allies, then maybe after a short time they went to war, then would sign peace treaties, etc., etc. Even now there are wars: for energy, for oil, for territories. But war is not always physical, carried out with weapons. Today there is the economic war and the financial war, which bring a nation to its knees without a single casualty. And this war is led undisturbed by groups and international powers, who with the power of money can do whatever they want, wherever they want. These topics, fascinating and disturbing, of which there is no mention in the media, must be deepened and interpreted. We will do so in the next chapters.

Chapter 8

Future Scenarios and Digitization

The web has already become indispensable in our lives. But we are still far from the real effects it will produce for us in the coming years. Digitization is still running side by side with paper, in many companies, especially in public companies of less evolved nations. How long will it take for the permanent abandonment of the paper-based system? Today we are well underway. In a few years, some digital instruments have won a now indispensable position. Can you imagine doing without Wikipedia, Facebook, YouTube, satellite navigators, google, smartphones and tablets with which you connect to the collective knowledge? No, right? Well, Wikipedia was born In 2001, Facebook in 2004, YouTube in 2005. The first smartphone dates back to 2007 and the first tablet to 2010. If you think back, the world before it seems like prehistoric time... but it was just yesterday. So how you can really think about paper books and printed encyclopedias as we know them today?

Technology is changing our lives and perhaps we have not even noticed it. Internet has come into our habits and as we move forward, we cannot do without it. It's taken hold of even the generations most reluctant to change. Very soon (we're speaking of a few years) robotic machines will supplant many activities that today are reserved for people. We are speaking about robots, those of the latest generation, the cognitive ones that learn while they work (like Apple's "Siri", Amazon's "Alexa", to be clear) that are going to make their entry in larger companies. The companies that produce them (mostly Japanese) are increasing their sales impressively every year and the sector is rapidly expanding. These robots replace the basic human activities as well as those of some white-collar workers (there is already talk of on-line lawyers and cybernetic columnists) and for each robot implemented in the company there is some person who is fired or not hired. They offer speed, lack of error and productivity at the highest level. They do not get sick, do not go on vacation, do not register with the union. They are fast and stupid but terribly efficient. They will replace millions of workers and knowledgeable employees, dramatically decreasing the tax revenue of the companies to the state. Every worker is in fact for a nation a huge (perhaps exaggerated) tax revenue. Which will disappear.

This is precisely why Bill Gates, creator of Microsoft and a billionaire, has raised the issue with a justified proposal to tax the robotized machines. To compensate for the losses of revenue. We fully agree. The automation and web world is moving inexorably forward with its facilitated online services and its amenities, which we are no longer willing to give up (travel tickets, e-commerce, making reservations, account management, management of long distance businesses…). The mentality has now been acquired, and we will never go back. Everything we do now through our pcs, smartphones or tablets seems normal, it is part of our habits and comfort. For those who come from the world in the 70s and 80s, when those who had power windows in their cars or the first portable phones were privileged and strutted around on the city streets, this continuous innovation is absorbed with difficulty. Many of us have already forgotten the queues at ticket offices, doubts about our vacations, the difficulty making reservations by phone, having to leave a deposit by credit card, traveling for meetings, the telephone booths with coins…Today we book our holidays in real time and we can even see the videos and explanatory photos of the locations, we study the comments of other users and we share everything and can do anything with a click from our smartphones. We study with online courses and seminars; we meet though live video instantly. This is no small feat. In a few months and a few years, given the speed of technological innovation, who knows what else we will be able to do while we sit on our couches. The Internet has put suddenly everyone in competition, everyone is visible, all exposed the judgment of users. Judgment which you can take you to the stars or reduce you to bankruptcy. So, the world companies are forced to improve their service and their availability to the customer to stay afloat. And this is not insignificant. It allows customers to get the best services in every field. To improve the experience and perception of everything. It allows the competent entrepreneurs able to be successful more easily.

If we transfer this in other fields, where this mentality is approaching, we understand how the social impact of internet has been devastating. For the greater good, obviously. I wondered recently, in a few years there will still beoffices? Or we all will work on the move or from our homes? Already some large companies have this setup, and more and more are offering their employees to "work from home" with an internet connection. Let's see how this transformation is changing businesses: think about banks. There are the traditional ones with tellers on the territory, employees, infrastructures, rents to pay, bills, signs and so on. And there are those "online". Management costs almost zero. Certainly, it is not the same thing, but we get the idea.

Ten years ago, today the largest companies by revenue did not even exist. Uber (taxi), Facebook, Airbnb (bed & breakfast), Google, Amazon, and thousands of other smaller companies. There exist because there is a web, they have no physical connotation or infrastructure. While traditional companies, once flourishing, are now in decline and disappearing with great speed. In the 80s the largest company was IBM. Does

The Basics of Financial Education

anyone remember it? The users of services are evolving while the providers of services are transforming themselves. Today, if you're not on the web you risk disappearing and however you are perceived as "old." The new generations of youth, the so-called millenials are ahead and they think so very differently from their fathers and their grandfathers. They share, they experience, use and utilize; they do not possess. They're called the generation of renting. Their smartphones work tirelessly, they receive and send messages, emoticons, videos and feelings. On average our teenagers live online for many hours a day and are constantly connected. Thanks to them, the spread of social networks is exponential (there is a new user every 18 seconds). Connections, instant messaging, new companies like Snapchat, Telegram, Whatsapp, Instagram... All these are used by them to convey emotions, images and opinions.

They are the new consumers: they compare prices, consider the best offers and buy online. Their store is the web. They want to share, get involved and be listened to: they use images more than words. And we must learn these new modes from them while at the same time transfer to them our wisdom and our experience. On them we have to rely on because they are the politicians, bankers, entrepreneurs and government officials of tomorrow. The future of the current and future generations is in their hands.

The Basics of Financial Education

Chapter 9

Money and Currency

Let's talk at this point about a basic concept that we must necessarily know money. Money is paper and in itself is worthless. But it is given a conventional value. Everything revolves around paper that is currency and is now a conventional instrument of payment. The principle was, and should be, that: you bring me goods with value (gold, silver, diamonds), in return I will give you the equivalent in currency that you can spend anywhere. This is the basis. Thus, currency was born, which replaced barter, and with it arose the first banks. Then with time everything went "down the drain." And it has taken a very dangerous deviation.

Today the State tells us: I am a sovereign State and I print money, as far as I want, and there's no longer anything to guarantee it, neither gold, silver or diamonds, or anything else. I am here to guarantee it, by the mere fact that I am a sovereign State, you have my word, I will pay my debts. It all started in 1971 when Richard Nixon (US Democratic president) released the dollar from equivalent value in gold voiding Bretton Woods agreements. In these international

The Basics of Financial Education

agreements rules were established for commercial and financial relations among the major countries in the industrialized world. A system of rules on currency and control over the monetary policies of nations was defined. This was the birth of an agreed upon monetary system to guarantee the monetary relationships among independent nation-states.

Before this 1971 event implemented by Nixon, in fact, for every printed dollar an equivalent amount in gold was deposited in the State Bank. And this took place in almost every country in the world. So, the world's money supply was an actual wealth, with a tangible remuneration. In case of collapse there was gold to guarantee the currency. After 1971 the money no longer had gold as a backup, everything has been liberalized and the money circulating in the world has become fictional: the currency has only a virtual value. This virtual wealth has since then multiplied to excess using a "leverage effect" and international investment banks have begun to develop complex financial instruments for a so-called "synthetic" finance with the issuance of derivatives. Financial derivatives are a terrible economic weapon and consist of a contract or a title whose value is based on the value of another title or another underlying contract. Hence the derivation concept. No one today is able to quantify the value of the derivatives in the world. One can build a derivative one every title and, on every contract, and on each derivative, you can build another extension, and so on with a devastating multiplying effect. A practical example of this is the subprime mortgages that triggered the economic crisis of 2007 in the USA. A loan agreement was contracted and on this were built derivative financial products repeatedly which worked as long as the loan was being paid by the borrower. If he no longer paying the installments, the whole castle of titles derived from the mortgage would collapse, sending into default the whole chain of products and so on. And those loans were not granted to solid borrowers, they were given to anyone, just to make an easy profit.

Another scandalous example is that of derivatives sold to public companies, some of which have found themselves in debt up to their necks. I forgot to say that everything stems from the fact that when a bank sells a derivative, the commission is very high. In the light of this many managers indebted the businesses or companies they managed, obtaining lavish commissions. Then they would lead the institution to bankruptcy, in debt up to their necks. Not everybody knows that even Nations have often signed with international business banks some very risky derivatives contracts which, while generating enormous losses, have had to be periodically renegotiated with a revenue loss of many billions of Euros or Dollars. These products are extremely risky, and they can earn a lot but also lose a lot. Free fantasy, aimed to the exasperated profit of these banking institutions,

The Basics of Financial Education

has led, and still leads, to the creation of newer and more risky instruments. Everything is fictitious, even the money you have in your pocket, even your savings in the bank. They are no longer guaranteed by anything.

Scenario number 1: as long as this state of affairs lasts all is well; until we can keep this phenomenon under control we do not have to worry. But now certainties are gradually slipping away, I think. Banks that fail, nations that collapse or are saved at the last minute, citizens' money put at risk, and so on and so forth. We'll see would happen (or will happen???) in a scenario where everything becomes out of control, as the phenomenon keeps inflating, inflating and inflating even more...

What is wealth after all? It should be a tangible property, a sure and tangible thing. Like gold or bricks. It is a real asset, not a fictitious one. Today this is no longer the case, there are the financial tycoons who base their wealth on paper assets, i.e., on stocks, bonds and derivative products. Until 1971 currencies were anchored to gold. There was, in the vaults of the central banks of States, an equivalent value in gold ingots. After 1971 it is clear that there has been a multiplication of wealth as money could be printed with no strings attached. And this downpour of money has meant that the economy has taken off (the wage increases, real estate skyrocketing, easy money). Do you think that the bank notes in your hands have a true value? It is something that is devaluating and devaluating more and more. So, consider currency (the dollar, the euro, etc.) as a temporary means to buy a good, a good that does not depreciate over time and that is not inflating freely without control.

This same currency placing system, called quantitative easing, borrowed from the USA, is taking place in Europe through the European Central Bank, which is printing and distributing Euros too thinly to the banks of the European system (but not the private sector and businesses directly). It is still banks with this function of intermediaries in the economy, which, acting as intermediaries, should lend money to businesses and citizens. But is this the case??? By separating the currency from any correspondence with precious metals (gold), it has become possible for modern states to print money "ad libitum" or at will. Are there debts to be paid? The US has made billions of dollars through quantitative easing, in Europe it has been the same for millions of Euros...This leads in theory to collapse. But are we sure that has not already occurred and that through the pumping of printed money we are not keeping alive an ailing economy? Let us meditate on these points. We are in the middle of an important and lasting economic depression.

What does all this mean for our portfolio? For our money? Simply that it is worth less every day. Let's use a public company as an example. There are 1,000 shares. I own 500 so I hold 50% of the company. If the company prints a thousand shares and distributes them, my ownership falls to 25% of the capital. And so on: the more shares (dollars or Euros) are printed the more my share of power (in our case, purchasing power) decreases. I think it's clear: the more money is printed and put in circulation, the more my money is worth less. So, it follows that my savings in money are worth less, as is my paycheck and my retirement fund. For this will potentially unleash inflation (i.e., devaluation of my purchasing power). Inflation is an occult tax. A tax we all unknowingly pay and from which the states benefit. If I cannot pay my electricity bill, I get cut off the. If the government cannot pay for energy? It prints money and pays. And indirectly we are charged. With inflation.

I have used a very basic terminology, I have simplified things and I apologize to those who already know them, but I wanted to make it clear once and for all how money works. Today, in our time, there are a thousand other more sophisticated products to multiply one's wealth. Think of the derivatives that we spoke about before. From 10 one can obtain one thousand, ten thousand, a million. This is the drugged economy of today. Then when the economy stops, and savers go to collect the money they have deposited in banks, they do not have anything because there never was anything. The multiplied money is purely fictional, figurative.

The Basics of Financial Education

This is so globalized and intertwined in the world economy that no one can say exactly how much money there is and how much of it is indeed real. If the system is running and playing all is well, but when it comes to default there is a collapse of the currency system. Considerations that should lead to a serious reflection.

Among other issues that we need to know is the one of rates. The newspapers are constantly speaking of an increase or decrease in the rate, announcing that the European Central Bank or the American Federal Reserve is varying the cost of money, that is, the rate on the euro or the dollar. We all hear this. But do we understand what it means? And its impact on us? If the cost of money rises, that is, the rates go up, it means that you will have two basic effects:

- if I have a mortgage to pay with a variable rate I will pay more because the installments will increase (the increase in the interest whereas the part of the capital remains unchanged)

- there will be an appreciation of the value of the currency. For example: if US interest rates increase, a dollar will cost more than a Euro i.e., exchange rates will rise against the Euro and in favor of the dollar. This is because there will be more interest in buying dollars because they will earn more. If you deposit it in the bank, it will pay a higher interest rate and therefore more money. On a macro level this has a considerable impact on the economy of country

- it will produce a higher inflation (we will see later what this really means)

- the currency will be stronger

- exports by country of origin, however, will decrease as the goods sold in that currency (and thus produced in that country) will be more expensive

- the relationship between that currency with all the other will vary, with all the possible and complex international aspects we can imagine. All these things are taken for granted, no one explains them. And the majority of citizens has the illusion of understanding, but then does not know how to translate those concepts into practice. He doesn't understand what the impact on his situation can be and, above all, is not aware of the opportunities that arise from those situations.

Chapter 10

Inflation and Hyperinflation

As we mentioned before, according to two schools of thought, there are two possible scenarios looming in the world:

Scenario A - We print money, and we worry about getting on; our descendants will deal with it. Scenario B - Hyperinflation and currency collapse.

What is happening around the world is that, with the globalized economy in deep crisis, we are trying to solve problems through massive injections of cash made by the main nations into their economic system. We reported that the USA began this with quantitative easing of billions and billions of dollars and the ECB in Europe is continuing this with the release of huge quantities of Euros to revitalize the banks and the real economy. Other sovereign States in the world are doing it on their own. What can we expect? Probably in the medium term an artificially induced economic recovery with a relapse in terms of inflation caused by overproduction of currency. What does all this cash surplus place on the market mean? Some economists and international observers assert that the world is heading towards a collapse of currencies. The collapse of markets, called "crashes", in fact have always existed and each of us have experienced one, even in the recent past. The stock market, the real estate market, the one of the currencies, and that of metals have always been characterized by cycles of ups and downs: the collapse of the real estate market and then its rise; the stock market crash and then its rebound...The worst is the possible collapse of currencies (the last we can remember - indeed that unfortunately we do not remember having erased every memory of it - is Germany from 1918 to 1923 with hyperinflation in Weimar Republic, where the bills were thrown into the street no longer having any value).

To frame the current scenario, I will try to bring some examples I have simply taken from Wikipedia so that each of you can rebut them, if you will. And you will see that these things are, not very distant in time, events of which you probably have never even heard, since there is no interest in disclosing them because they make people because they reflect. They make you think carefully. I ask you of you the effort to read them, although I have tried to simplify the examples and the numbers.

The Basics of Financial Education

History has known many cases of depreciation, or hyperinflation, let us mention just a few, starting from a far back:

- Athens, at the end of the Peloponnesian War (404 BC)

- Ancient Rome, under the reigns of numerous emperors, from Caracalla (212 AD) to Diocletian (AD 280)

- The American Colonies under the Continental Congress in 1781

- France 1790-1796

- Austria, Hungary, Poland and Russia after the first world war

- Brazil between 1970 and 1990 where they officially adopted almost endless series of currencies (réis, cruzeiro, cruzeiro novo, cruzado, novo cruzado, re cruzeiro and finally, since 1994, the cruzeiro real)

- Colombia, which received from the infamous drug trafficker Pablo Escobar the proposal of having all national debts paid off with the proceeds of drug trafficking in exchange for immunity for the Colombian drug cartels

- Germany that, in the countries that it invaded during World War II, imposed the "mark of occupation", that is an artificial higher exchange rate with respect to the defeated countries (who in turn were devaluated)

- Argentina, which officially never repaid its foreign shareholders of its bonds in 2002 (and this I remember work-wise! When in the bank there were dozens of desperate investors!)

As we write this, there is a terrible inflation in Venezuela, which is nearing the measure of ten million percent!! We are talking about one of the richest countries of the world in terms of oil. And precisely to compensate for the lower revenues due to the very low price of oil, the government continued to print more money bringing inflation to its peak. The fall is exponential. For months, Venezuelans have been going grocery shopping more and more full of banknotes to buy those few essential items that are still available. The situation is very serious and is a typical case of hyperinflation caused by printing huge amounts of money. It is not theory or history; it is happening today.

But the most spectacular hyperinflation in recent history, for which we have the most appropriate statistics, occurred in Germany from 1919 to the end of 1923. Let me recount it briefly.

The Basics of Financial Education

The Weimar Hyperinflation

At the outbreak of the First World War, in 1914, to cope with the huge war effort, Germany abolished the gold convertibility of the mark (just as Nixon did in the US in 1971). The people in proximity of imminent war, out of fear, with from banks gold coins for a value of 100 million marks. The government chose to finance itself by printing more money and, until the end of the conflict, the amount of money in circulation had quintupled. Like a time, bomb, financial imbalances exploded after five years in all their tremendous drama. Inflation reached impressive levels, and the last two years (1921 - 1923) the so-called "Weimar hyperinflation" broke out. The Mark came to be worth one billionth (1 / 1,000,000,000,000) of its worth nine years before (1914).

The victorious nations of the World War decided to charge Germany the costs of war borne by them. Without any regard to the gold reserves that were supposed to ensure the currency, Germany continued to print paper money until the debt was paid off, which caused the rapid further depreciation of the mark. During hyperinflation, the paper mark was produced in vast quantities: there were also cuts of 100,000,000,000,000 DM (one hundred thousand billion).

Hundreds of domestic factories, converted to printing facilities, were printing new bills day and night. Public and private printers emitted rivers of marks that were not worth the price of the paper on which were etched. More than 30 factories were producing paper and 133 companies were printing money. In total, 524 trillion marks were issue (a gazillion has 18 zeros), which were added to another 700 trillion to tackle the economic crisis.

In 1923 the German government was forced to pay the employees' salaries on a daily basis, who would then hurry to buy any merchandise they could before seeing their money literally between their hands. On November 15th, 1923, one US dollar bought 4.2 trillion German marks and, to buy a kilogram of bread in Germany, it took more than a kilo of banknotes. Wheelbarrows full of paper currency were needed to buy an egg or a tram ticket. In this dramatic situation, the people returned to doing without money; in fact, they returned to barter and banknotes were used to turn on the heaters. The highest denomination of a banknote during German hyperinflation was 100 million billion (100,000,000,000,000) marks! It's an extreme case, but it gives you the idea. Hyperinflation consists of a huge and continuous increase in prices due to the huge input of money, which loses its value day by day.

The Basics of Financial Education

The economy is becoming impoverished visibly, especially impoverishing the weakest, because during hyperinflation it is the most cunning who take advantage of the situation. The losers are - at first - those who have a fixed income, such as employees, while temporarily saving those who can adapt theirs wages to the continuous rise in prices (e.g., the retailers). Frequent, recent and current cases of hyperinflation are repeating in world. Believe us, there are dozens and dozens of cases around the world, just read up. Do it out of curiosity. And all these crises were generated from the same cause: the printing of money without any real equivalent to guarantee it. Here are some of the most recent, striking cases of hyperinflation; they are among the latest relating to the most popular countries (source Wikipedia). Look at the inflation rates reached in percentage points:

- Russia 210% in 1991/1992

- Italy 37.5% in 1943/1945 and 18% in 1979/1980

- Mexico 833% in 1993/1994

- Germany (see above) 29,500% in 1920/1923

- Argentina 196% in 1898/1990

- China 4,209% in 1947/1949

The Basics of Financial Education

- Greece 11,288% in 1942/1945

... and many other cases ...

As mentioned above in Italy, in the 70s, there was a period of high inflation (18%) and I remember it. Many families and my father too, during periods of high inflation, made their fortunes by buying properties with a loan then finding after many years to have a good with a very high value paying loan installments with a ridiculous face value (Here is an opportunity!). I also experienced this situation firsthand many years ago when I paid the final installment of a loan contracted many years by prior my parents (70s). I remember that it was equivalent to the price of a movie ticket. Yet when that loan was contracted the rate was very expensive. But this is the effect of inflation.

I reported this information because I hope to have provided some unknown information to the majority of readers, especially to young people who have not experienced times of inflation. To ask you to reflect on what is happening right now in the economy and global finance and, in my opinion, is kept deliberately concealed and is completely underestimated. An excessive amount of circulating currency is one of the main factors of inflation. It is a real danger and is powered by excessive money printing by national and central banks. This continuous emission meets the needs of

The Basics of Financial Education

liquidity of some economic entity, like the state, disregarding the consequences - for the entire system and for citizens - of an excessive mass of money in circulation. The financing of a State should take place by collecting taxes and the issuance of government bonds that are purchased and with which they obtain money. These are the main sources of financing of a nation. Instead, it is financed, as well as in the above ways, by printing new money.

Inflation creates an advantage and a great opportunity for those who have debts, since the value of these decreases are due to the devaluation. The continuous loss of purchasing power of money (typical during periods of inflation) urges citizens to get rid as soon as possible of the cash they have received, helping to accelerate even more the phenomenon of inflation; it triggers a vicious circle. Inflation always has a serious impact on the balance of political system. The uncertainty about the value of money is transmitted to all economic activities, discouraging investment, with serious consequences at the national income level, on employment and the real economy. Currently, the monetary policies of the major economic blocs (US, Europe, Japan, etc.) are intertwined and, perhaps, imitate each other, having global reciprocal influences. I am intentionally omitting to mention dramatic scenarios that some international economists and opinion leaders are citing on the huge phenomenon of inserting of currency in the markets. If you want, check up on this.

Back to us: what happens in our daily lives? When a family cannot make ends meet, they begin to borrow against their credit card and postpone paying the debt; they pay after pay fifteen days, a month, and they fact use consistently money not they haven't got, but they will refund in the future. The same has been done and is being done by sovereign states, banks and all financial entities. All use a wealth they do not have, a fictitious wealth this remains so until someone says enough, let's call in the debt. And then it all falls apart, there is a default. The family goes into default, but not the state: the state is saved. It can print more money or issue other securities and pay its debts. And we have said that increasing the amount of money in circulation makes citizens poorer for their money is always worth less (growth of the money supply and inflation). The more money that circulates, the less it is worth. A rule to keep in mind.

If you transpose this principle to currency and to debts contracted by nations and you multiply it throughout the globalized world, you will realize that today we are living in fictitious money and wealth, simply by postponing payments of debt. Many industrialized countries are burdened by a huge public debt. If borrowers were asked to pay off their debts completely what happen? The failure of the state and therefore all citizens. And what happens when there is a currency collapse? The result is that the money becomes (see examples of Germany or Venezuela) worthless paper off wiping out its value in the hands of citizens. The only surviving goods that survive are material (real estate) or precious (gold, silver and diamond) but this doesn't mean that it won't take dozens of years to restore the original values.

Speaking of examples, if two friends had an availability of 1 million dollars each, one invested in paper assets (stocks, bonds, titles) and one bought a real estate property, in the presence of a currency collapse the only one that will retain something in his hand is the one who had purchased the property that does not dissolve into nothing but remains usable and tangible (regardless of its current or resale value). The only real valuable asset is tangible and that has an intrinsic value: gold, silver, diamonds or brick. From the dawn of civilization man has seen precious metals as a source of wealth. Gold is limited in the world, as is silver, and they are all recognized as valuable assets, which survive through every crisis, every time. What would happen to our savings? And our pension funds? This is why investing in physical assets is not wrong. Although maybe the eventual, and likely, collapse will not happen in our generation, it is good foresight to preserve our possessions. With these considerations, a bit extreme if you will, I hope I have not given rise to fear or immediate concerns. These phenomena act slowly, they will

The Basics of Financial Education

not happen tomorrow morning. The world economy is so intertwined and interdependent that any monetary crisis will not happen just in one country: we will see the warning signs beforehand. But will be able to recognize those signals if we have reached a good financial education and we will be able to read events.

Let me speculate on a science fiction theory at this point, which many authors and reporters (increasingly) describe in their books. It is said that the world is ruled by a financial oligarchy which controls the financial and economic power, and thus also politics. There is talk of the Bilderberg club and the Trilateral Commission (fascinating topics that we hope to treat soon in other publications). I would like to make some mention of them here since some people have begun to talk about them. The Bilderberg Club, founded by David Rockefeller (as was the Trilateral Commission) is a committee that, since 1954, gathers once a year in absolute secrecy in an overprotected and unapproachable place, to decide, they say, the economic and political future of the world. The name comes from the hotel where the group initially gathered in the Netherlands. Never no one has been able to approach them, nor has any reporter or journalist been able to film or document what happens inside this meeting. The founders and main exponents are characters of international caliber who hold the power, not political, but in the financial world through major international investment banks. Together with

The Basics of Financial Education

business managers, opinion leaders, lobbyists as well as unknown seeds; but no one knows the twists and turns of all of these exponents. Although some ideas, by consulting the lists of invitees, can be formulated.

Compared to these lobbies politics, corporations and nations are at a lower level (I think we have understand this at this point in the book!). Daniel Estulin deals with the Bilderberg case in such an egregious way in his book "The Bilderberg Club", which I highly recommend.

In these secret meetings, Estulin states in his book, financial wars and crises are decided (to be seen later), where they should take place, which economy to bring to its knees, which to support, which political group to break down, and so on all the destinies, at the macro level, of the western world. And these broad international designs are planned at a table many years prior to their implementation. The power of money at its maximum expression. By reading the names of the participants one understands a lot of politics and of the international plots.

Getting back to the design, which was mentioned before, these international oligarchies would have coordinated, for many years ago in the meetings held periodically, to take over everything gradually. Take control of everything. And they are already at a good point in their plan. At first, they trigger silent financial wars (to be seen later), they intervene on this or that economy of this or that country sending it into an economic crisis (almost by default), and then, with prices down to a minimum, they buy all the most important assets of that country. Companies, industries, luxury real estate, economic activities that, when they determine in the same way the "rebirth", will have a much higher value and will ensure to the group complete control of the economy and finance. These oligarchies, who hold the power of printing money in the world, have figured out that sooner or later the currency collapse (natural or induced) is inevitable, and they are buying all the physical assets that constitute the world's wealth. Some are even arguing that the rise of alternative popular movements in the European and world politics, is facilitated artfully to charge the same movements, when they are in power, with the collapse that is on its way, and then delete them forever from the political scene. Unfortunately, those who control the money in the world can do everything and determine anything.

Everything depends on money. These entities place themselves above of the nations, above politics, above everything. They are the producers and managers of money and wealth and can do whatever they want in anywhere in the world. The only thing they cannot control is nature and climatic and atmospheric events. I leave you to comment on this scenario. Does it seem lik political fiction? Read up on

The Basics of Financial Education

it, widen your view of the international world, read something on the subject, make up your own an idea. We will discuss this topic in the near future because it is too important to know the details. We will bring it back as simple news, leaving the reader to judge. I am sure that you will ask yourselves some questions.

Chapter 11

New Forms of Warfare

Today there are two types of wars or rather two different ways of making war. The traditional one, made up of soldiers, weapons, ammunition, bombs, special forces and drones. And the invisible, more lethal one: the war of money. Today you can bring a sovereign state to its knees without even firing a blow, but by simply attacking it from a financial point of view. Through the banks and international transactions, you can undermine the entire economy of a country.

The invisible war of the money is piloted. Let's go back to the currency: the worst-case scenario that could ever happen is a big explosion, the big currency collapse, which we hope will never happen. Having said all this, however, we live in the risk of a colossal collapse of all the western economies, since the latter are based on a dummy multiplier effect of wealth whose cause is the indiscriminate issuance of circulating money. We see and manage an asset that does not really exist. Member states support the markets and pay their bills with the input of printed money and distribute money to people in forms of assistance to not work.

The Basics of Financial Education

How long can all this last? Common sense tells us that someone will eventually pay the bill. And it will be us: citizens, investors and savers. When there is the potential collapse, unless a solution is found that for now, we do not see on the horizon, we will have no certainties. We have seen that when a company or a bank fails there are no more safeguards to protect you and you lose your money (we are seeing this, right?). If we don't learn to think observing the world from above, but we live immersed in our micro reality drugged by false information, by false promises and artificial reassurances, we will have some big disappointments.

The world is ruled by individuals who are under the influence of powerful groups that manage the financial power (modern weapons). Economies are distorted by artificial wealth; nations avoid collapse by printing money. The only resource we have is money. Inflation, deflation, depression: all phenomena that do not follow their natural course, but are manipulated with artificial financial instruments (derivatives, quantitative easing, bailouts, and so on). But the reality is that now no one is able to control global finance and that the process is out of control. There remains great uncertainty about whether, and possibly when, this will happen and how the effects can be contained. History is full of these examples, as we have seen before, that we have now forgotten. I am, thanks to my mental training, optimistic about the future, but I couldn't not mention this news and this vision of the world

The Basics of Financial Education

economy. Then, if I will have managed to make the reader think, to make him understand what surrounds him, I'll have met my goal. This is also financial education; indeed, it is its essence.

The Basics of Financial Education

Chapter 12

Crisis as Opportunity

The ages are riddled with crises. During crises the greatest wealth is created, the brightest minds emerge and the strongest survive. Crises are lasting or fleeting, deep or superficial, real or imagined. The economy is cyclical, and we must learn to take advantage of the opportunities that appear negative and yet hide rich business opportunities. Every crisis is full of opportunities. In the last 20 years we endured many a crisis.

All announced these crises, at their vigil, and they were announced as apocalyptic…when in actuality they were only in part or with consequences much less worrisome than those announced by newspapers in the days before. And many people speculated on these clamours and became richer. While the average citizens, frightened by catastrophic announcements and newspapers, withdrew into themselves without grasping the opportunities. Here I am talking about investments in the stock market, obviously.

The Basics of Financial Education

But what does crisis mean?

Being worse than before?

Seeing black for the future?

The crisis of 1929 lasted 25 years and is usually the crisis compared to the current one, which began in 2007/2008 with the bankruptcy of the investment bank Lehman Brothers' and the subprime mortgage crisis in the United States. So, now we are in 2019, the crisis has been continuing already for about 12 years. Will we be able to hold on for another 10-15 years? We might as well focus on how to take advantage of this state of crisis and seize the opportunities it offers. Every economic condition presents opportunities. No one will help you understand how to take advantage of them or how to capture the favorable moments: we always be kept in a state of tension by media that will keep us fearful and concerned about doing anything. Those who control the monetary system also controls the education and information systems, and we have seen that this will not facilitate us in any way. However, the web is an unstoppable cyclone and control or no control, lobbies or oligarchies, if you will, the information circulates and is free to be acquired and interpreted by all.

To look to the future and understand the present, you have to learn from past. Change comes through the knowledge

The Basics of Financial Education

that, if you're reading this book, you're ready to learn because it's in your best interest. Young people, who have been compared to "boomerangs" because they return to live with their parents, are our future but are not able to settle down: too much unemployment and too few opportunities. You study, you get a diploma or degree and then stop in limbo, before finding a good work. Those years on hold have devastating effects on the maturation of a future pension fund, as well as the skills and experience that you need to acquire, and which cannot be delayed. One leans on the family for support. This is where we must not lose time waiting for a job. It is in this phase that everyone should strive to grow and improve, beyond family, school or beyond traditional studies.

The computer evolution is working in favor of those with an open-mind and who are looking towards the future. The traditional balances are collapsing. Those who had power and who reasoned "old style", are losing it, though they are trying to keep it with reckless actions. The new is advancing powerfully and aims to undermine all that is not innovative. If you are young you have to reflect deeply and understand that the state will not take care of you. You'll have to fend for yourself. And above all you have to keep up with the new, not with old. And invent a road by abandoning the idea of the permanent position.

The Basics of Financial Education

How does the population move during a deep crisis such as this one? The rich increase their wealth. The other ranks fall lower. The upper middle class descend to the middle level and the middle class becomes poorer. Those who were barely surviving cross the poverty line. Why does this happen? Because the rich have the money and the goods and can make the work money in their favor, really use the assets and create income. The others, the middle classes, may have the assets, but they mainly support themselves with their work. They think that owning a house is a source of security and wealth, which is not the case if they live in that house. It costs more or less the same that it would cost you to rent a house (including taxes and maintenance) plus you have your money locked down. It is better if you bought the house with a mortgage and you're paying the installments, and using the cash you would have used to buy it (without getting a mortgage) and have it invested in another way. Maybe buying another house and renting it.

You have capital if you own additional assets, otherwise you've pinned your only wealth down in an asset which you live in and still have to pay for. You can use goods to make income. In our world we are very lucky, more so than in the past. Information abounds, of every kind and nature, on the web, in newspapers and so on. But that information must be compiled and processed through knowledge. Only then can it

The Basics of Financial Education

be fruitful. Otherwise, it remains on the newsprint and passes through our brains without leaving anything.

We have to become aware that we are slaves of money. Everything in our society revolves around money. It is a good for trade or to measure the well-being of everyone, which is not controlled by the individual, but is adjusted in value, by the state. The state in fact, can modulate the wealth and well-being of each citizen through the deprivation of money. Let me explain.

On the salary or income of a citizen, the state intervenes to subtract money from their pockets through 3 elements: taxes, inflation and induced debt.

The induced debt is an element of which we are becoming slaves. I pay you your salary, I will halve it (or more) with the withholding taxes at the source, and so to live, I force you into debt because otherwise you'll make not it. And with your debt you feed the banks that are in turn inside the circuit. That is, when the salary is not enough, because the fees and taxes erode it completely, the citizen turns to debt: installment loans, credit cards, revolving credit cards, consumer financing and uses the wealth of others which he does not possess. And often he runs up the credit limit to a point of no return. Am I saying stupid things? What are the most publicized products today if not personal loans? Financial companies try to hook us in through banks, the internet, telephone contacts, emails, personalized letters: all to make us ask for consumer loans. So, you take the loan, you use it for consumption (futile assets, depreciable, of rapid fruition) and then you are left with the debt. For 36,48,72,120 months. And you become poorer because you are more into debt.

The new slavery of our time is debt, the debt for livelihood or consumerism. Not the debt for investment, which will be discussed later. If the debt is used for an investment (e.g., to buy a house and pay in installments), I am creating future wealth. If I use the debt for consumption, as corporations lead me to do--that is buy a depreciable asset such as a TV, a car, a vacation--or use it to pay for current charges or fees, I indebt myself without a logical end. I become poorer and slip downwards. This phenomenon, in the US, is much ahead of Europe. It is as if the population were shackled with debt to banks and financial entities, and taxes to the state. What remains is just enough to the people to survive on. But taxation (we shall see later) and inflation make everyone poorer and slaves to the system. A people in debt is weaker and more controllable. The profits of the debts of citizens go to the usual bankers and international financiers. And all are more vulnerable and slide downward.

Chapter 13

Labor and the End of Permanent Jobs

Another of the important current topics is the lack of employment and work. But how do we Italians understand work? Or rather, how have they have made us understand work in the past 50 years? Mainly as a permanent job. The South European Nations were the most amazing factories of clerks, entire generations instructed and educated to worship the permanent position. For decades the party bureaucrats have set up permanent positions in every State and State-controlled body, concentrating recruitment this way and that, but always only in the interest of creating basins of votes for their re-election. How many places are redundant in Public Administration? And how many useless bodies exist that erode citizens' wealth? And while, in the private sector technological computerization has eroded jobs and made thousands of middle-aged workers obsolete, in the State all this It does not occur. We continue to maintain armies of public clerks, some of great value, but many others are absentee workers. All disgruntled and with poor productivity. But then what should they do if they are not given anything to do? If everything is adrift?

The Basics of Financial Education

Here lies the big problem to solve. You cannot fire, but you should cut and reorganize. But does anyone appear to be doing this? Everything is continuing with the same system. Today, with all our illusions and certainties collapsed, what do our young people have to believe in? In a Europe where not even people in their 50s have job security? The employment crisis leads us to ask ourselves how each of us should be geared for the future, having already noted that there is no longer the permanent position and the jobs that are left are not risk-free. The fall of the strength of unions and the loss of guarantees from the State and parties, the elimination (or near elimination) of our hope for a pension hope for those who start a business, mean that today only he who invests in himself, the "self-made man", will be able to make it. No longer able to count on any help from the State, means that one must invest in one's education first of all, then on one's relational capabilities, one's knowledge of languages and new technologies. To try find one's own path.

Reasoning seriously on job market leads us to not kid ourselves with illusions. When my generation started, those of us in our fifties, there were many more opportunities. Apart from the permanent positions one could steer towards information technology, which was in its infancy, and in many areas that were still receptive. Moreover, there was less competition. Today the world has changed for the worse. There are less jobs, job offers, very few opportunities and the

The Basics of Financial Education

GNP is zero or almost. What does it mean? That if there is no economic growth, and there is no investment, no new jobs are created. You have probably heard this many times. Moreover, the employment that is available is at risk (the advent of robotics, digitization, which we talked about earlier). I know many former leaders in their 50s and 60s who had mega offices with hundreds of people to coordinate, secretaries and various company benefits, who today (not having set aside a single euro - see lack of financial education) are forced to beg for a place as accountants or blue-collar workers. Or, if they were farsighted and built something, they live consuming their accumulated assets.

Europe needs entrepreneurs, not clerks. And yet the training process of a student is still for those looking for a permanent position. Schools, universities, financial ignorance, looking for "the so-called" safety in any public or private employment, to this we have been steered. But all this is over. As we wait for someone to notice and modify this at a government level, this training of clerks and not of entrepreneurs, each must fend for himself. By beginning his training process (as I have suggested). Each person should build his own way.

Do you know how many paper resumes are received by companies and banks every day? Thousands upon thousands...And those in digital format? Thousands upon thousands...You may have noticed that today private companies, such as banks, are no longer hiring and have thousands of redundancies, as the newspapers say. And even if a small position for a clerk should materialize who do you think they would hire? I've been a headhunter for a bank, so I will explain to you how this works. They hire:

1. Protected categories: they cost less and fulfill the legal requirement (many are not real invalids; they have disability status for various reasons which not serious and can be fully active)

2. Those with recommendations: in your opinion between the leaders, the Board of Directors, the shareholders, the best customers there is no one who is indicated by anyone? The "recommended" are thousands.

3. Given the choice between the candidates, they select the one with two degrees, international masters, who speaks five languages and maybe graduated at Harvard!! Because young people with these credentials abound.

I remember, after a selection, I hired a guy who was a phenomenon and that had more titles than the CEO!! Although my opinion is that titles are absolutely not a guarantee of great capacities. There are other qualities needed to emerge, not school qualifications. But for recruitment purposes, given several candidates with equal qualifications,

The Basics of Financial Education

titles are important, and how. For companies it is best to hire those with the highest level of qualifications and experience, since the cost is the same. So, if you want to compete with the highly qualified and desirable for this type of job, you must begin to study hard and that's what we are here for. But even if you plan to do something else or start own your business you need to study even harder and instruct yourself financially. So, invest in your education.

Financial education, as we have said, gives you a set of basic skills and in-depth knowledge of economy, finance, banks, property, entrepreneurship, taxation and so on. In any case, these matters will be useful for living, because you will have the ability to look at the market with more attentive eyes for opportunity. Opportunities that exist especially in a economic crisis like the current one, but it is very hard to see and identify them.

Digitization, if you missed it, has turned and is indeed turning the world around with double-digit advances. Would you open today a roadside shop (cost of the premises, personnel to hire, merchandise, stockroom, accountant, signs, permits, opening and closing times, and... need I go on ...)? Customers of a traditional store are fewer and fewer. Today, those who savoring the pleasure, comfort and convenience of buying on-line do not go back. So, a store or a business should be opened "on-line", not on the street. Besides, your customers will not be only those in the city or neighborhood where you live but, potentially, they will be customers from around the world who can buy with just one click. All you need is an attractive and new product, then open a site... Personally I have been studying for a long time the digitization and online sales techniques that are completely different from traditional ones. And they are already the present.

Many young people already in this business are the invisible web millionaires. Youngsters who operate through websites and blogs, marketers, who have become rich and powerful having been the first to explore the potential of internet. These areas are already well advanced, but they still offer room for growth. Be careful, I'm not saying it's easy, because it's not, but the advantage of these activities on the web is that require low investments and are easily accessible to all. Let's read up on what the web offers and on related activities. There are seminars, courses, websites and books, which even in our country are easily reachable and can put the most resourceful in the condition to independently startup an entrepreneurial activity. The Americans have produced texts and courses aplenty.

Another area to be explored is that of relational communication. Our relationships are and remain the cornerstone of our whole existence. From the time of cave men to today, technologies or no technologies, contact with other human beings is the starting point for success. If we can govern interpersonal relationships, guiding the relationship, we will have success in our hands. Whether we are dealing with a head of state, or the man on the street, our relational power will make the difference. Everywhere we go and whatever work we do, we relate to our fellow human beings. Coaching, NLP, communication, financial education: all materials that we need to deepen further. If we open our minds with study, then we have to insert some content into them and the content is for us what allows us to work, to settle down, to progress and to reach economic independence. For every street is smoothed out for a good communicator. We might as well invest in this for us and for our children. Where there are no innate qualities, you can learn everything with perseverance and study.

In conclusion, being tied down to a permanent position, with no more guarantees and with a fixed salary, are not things that I hope for young people who are on average much more brilliant and creative any other class of teenagers in the world.

Instead, we can do much for ourselves individually, investing on ourselves and our capacities. Cyclically governments, nations, continents go up and down the economic ladder (just look at history in a more diluted temporal arc), so what is done is nothing more than a return of some past that recurs cyclically. This is why it is important to study the political and

The Basics of Financial Education

socio-economic events of the past to understand the present and to try to predict the future.

Chapter 14

The Fiscal Robbery

Paying taxes is right, it is the moral duty of every citizen. How many times have we heard this spiel on television and newspapers, enunciated by heads of government or the presidents of the Republic? Let us pause for a moment. They have so inculcated in this sentence in our brains that for many of us it is almost a dogma. But it is true to a certain extent. Paying taxes is right up to a limit. For me, the limit is that the state cannot earn more than a citizen earns. That is: if you earn $1,000, the maximum limit (which is already quite high) is 50%. So, I can pay, (in my view) $500. It shouldn't be, or rather it is not fair, nor morally or socially correct, for me to work and have a silent partner who collects more I do, while doing nothing and without bringing me any support or service. Every citizen is a minority shareholder of his income.

Let's look at a high salary, for example. Suppose you pay a tax rate of 50%. Plus we pay taxes on products and services that we use, the car, the fuel, on the house, on rent, on utility bills, on the insurance policies that we have, and so on...So if my income is 1000 Dollars, and 50% is withheld by the state at the source, I am left with 500 Dollars. From these 500 Dollars I must also deduct all the other indirect taxes I quoted earlier. I will be left with 250/300 Dollars of the initial 1000 I earned through my work. Everything else then is taken by the State directly (at the source) or indirectly (with indirect taxes). But is all this moral? It is socially just? Or is it a cash theft fine plain and simple?

I cannot help but talk about taxes. Of the tax robbery and fiscal dictatorship to which honest citizens and pensioners are subject to. In addition, in some country's taxes are levied without receiving anything in return from the State. And I cannot help but be objective and critical. And yes, I'd like to dispel a lot of clichés!!! The first is that it is right to pay taxes, without reservation. It is true. It is a civic duty. But up to what limit? Or do we want to be subject to to this constant blackmail that seems to have no end? The State, if it wants to, does not pay anybody, it postpones paying its debts, it pays when it is convenient and provides services in return, which are sometimes marginal and of low quality.

The citizen, if he is late on the payment of his taxes for even a single day you find himself more indebted by interest, penalties, foreclosures, all the way to an administrative distraint or even a legal mortgage on the house. Are you sure that not there should be no limit to the greed of the State? And who fixes the high limit beyond which they cannot go?

The Basics of Financial Education

Those who want us to believe the message that paying taxes without objecting is our duty for the common good no longer find me in favor. You have to pay taxes, but much what we contribute is used in a questionable way or is used for doing favors to lobbyists or corporations or goes into the politicians' pockets and not as it should by returning to the citizen or decreasing the public debt. And if the public debt does decrease in a period with interest rates as "low" as the right now, we will never come out ahead. Instead, the public debt of the States continues to rise each year. And the wastes are not cut. And the authorities are not suppressed. And they continue to eat big time.

With a real tax burden, I am referring this time to Europe, at 73% (with the reasoning of before we come to this absurd percent) do not talk to me about moral duty to pay taxes!! Nor talk about services offered on taxation. We are paying now, during our lifetime, the mistakes and debts contracted by previous administrations as if we had accepted the legacy of a grandparent who left us in debt. The grandpa has squandered, gambled, stolen, gone philandering and I have to pay his debt. It's like living in a condo and, in addition to paying the expenses for monthly services, we are forced to pay the debts incurred by past administrators who have run away with the cash.

The Basics of Financial Education

Let me give you an example. Long ago, the United States were a tax-free country or with a low taxation (even today there are some foreign countries that have a tax rate of around 10/15%). Then, gradually, to finance various internal and international wars, the taxes increased. In addition, for the government to collect the taxes it had to wait for citizens to pay them spontaneously at the end of the year, as they do now with us free professionals and companies. So here is the big gimmick, eventually adopted by all: the American government introduced in 1943 the "current tax payment act" that allowed the State to be paid before the workers. In this way, by withholding taxes at the source, the state takes its money first only after pays the worker and the citizen; it allows him to take the proceeds of his work and his fatigue after it is done. At first this was done with a bearable tax burden, then gradually with a greater arrogance and greed, and now it has gotten to the point that the state is taking our money at the source and manages tax rates, deductions, and scams to deprive a citizen of an important part (and absolutely excessive) of his income from work. The same happens with all other personal property. It's a gigantic and continuous cash robbery, which increases more and more as the state becomes more and more needy and the politicians more and more greedy.

On the other hand, if you have debts then you must pay, and our country is debt-ridden and in the hands of an oligarchy that impoverishes us every day of our belongings. What future is there if these are the scenarios? If public debt is not slashed at a time like this with rates to a minimum? If citizens must forever pay a debt that will never be extinguished, and that actually grows more and more at the expense of each common sense? Maybe run away to other shores in less greedy States, as are doing more and more entrepreneurs, is a legitimate aspiration. The same goes for thousands of entrepreneurs who are going to countries overseas, where tax rates allow them to be more competitive and enjoy the legitimate profit of their businesses.

So never mind the social or moral conscience... taxes are fair up to a certain limit, beyond that, no. Beyond this they are immoral and, as far as I'm concerned, they represent a theft to the citizen. It is depressing to see that our best entrepreneurs (who could give work to our children) emigrate every day to other less greedy countries and taxes that the rich are leaving to live in tax havens. But you would do that? If instead of paying 70%, you were asked only a flat 15% of tax rate? Would you not go? In addition, this huge cash robbery against us cannot reach higher rates (but not necessarily...because some European States risk having to put more money to save the banks!). And for this reason, the State is looking for, always in my opinion, where there are pockets of money available (e.g., the pension funds or savings accounts). Greedy State. Be careful! Where there is cash, the state eventually will put its hands on it!

Politics

What is politics if not the commitment to the "polis", namely the community? The concept now appears completely distorted by those who make politics a profession aimed at maintaining power and personal enrichment or collateral. Each reader has hundreds of examples of mismanagement and looting by politicians. Do we want to get rid of it once and for all? Do we want to eventually elect, in turn and for fixed periods, people who serve the interests of the community? As long as there are fat cows, you can be tolerant, but when there is a persistent and relentless crisis as we are experiencing, one tightens his belt and whips the guilty!

Chapter 15

Bank Lending

Knowing your credit and therefore the banks, means knowing the system to obtain money. And without money nothing is done. You cannot start a business, you cannot buy a property, you cannot even buy a machine or a car, you cannot do anything. Or you have to ask your friends and family for help, a very difficult road that forces you to be grateful to someone forever. The money is obtained by the banks through credit. But to get credit must know the principles of financial education and you must understand how to act and how to behave towards the financial institutions. Creating a financial credibility means being labeled as solvent by the system and then being able to start your own path towards investment and income. Without this, unless you are capitalized, you cannot hope for success and an improvement in our financial condition. You have to know what to say in a meeting with the director of a bank or consultant and you have to know what he wants to hear. You have to put him in the position to want to give you a credit line. It's all about refining your knowledge of credit lines and banks, in order to talk as equals and not appear naive. The higher the technical content of the interview the more you will be respected and accommodated in your requests for financing.

The bank cannot wait to and finance you and earn some money, but under certain conditions. And you cannot wait to be granted a loan or funded to undertake your project. Between these two requirements, which coincide, there is a whole world to explore and get to know. Our society is based on capitalism and the economy is managed and supported by banks. Banks are the primary filter of each relationship and before each deal. To get credit I have to know my limits and my financial chances. I need to know what the characteristics and qualities are I have to put to work in order to obtain financing. Once the banking world was nebulous and hermetic; today it is easier enter into it.

However, while during the phases of economic expansion it is easy to obtain funding, as things stand now banks concession valves are shut tightly. Newspapers seem to assert the opposite, central banks are granting money very thinly, the rates are negative in Europe, and the banks, to hold your money in the European Central Bank are paying (0.40%) instead of receiving interest, and yet they are not financing. The reason for this fear and narrowness is found mainly in the fact that the indices and parameters that banks must follow are stricter. The issue of substandard and doubtful loans or NPL (non-performing loans - the problem loans and

The Basics of Financial Education

receivables which will no longer be recouped from concessions of the past) has maximum attention. All the flaws of major European banks are emerging. Many are on the verge of default. In this scenario, to get credit, I have to prove a solidity and a capacity to produce concrete and lasting income. We no longer get credit on the basis of solid guarantees. Therefore, to get funding, we must be prepared, reliable according to banking principles, communicative and skillful negotiators. It is essential to build a financial credibility, moving into a complicated area, where the information is not accessible to all, where there are financial databases, where we are definitely classified and where we need to prove to be good borrowers.

Now more than ever, with interest rates near zero, with a good probability of inflation, with asset prices (real estate and businesses) so low, it pays to invest with money I have borrowed. Never before have all indicators been so favorable for undertaking investments for the future. Real estate costs less, property owners are more willing to negotiate, commercial activities (but be careful what you choose ...) can be purchased at a low price, there are no longer the exorbitant sums required to take over a business as was before. So, it's time to move if you have good ideas. But you have to be able to have them financed. And in Europe there isn't the culture and the ability to finance good ideas and projects of capable young people. Unlike in the United States where, if there had been this attitude, the large companies that dominate the world business would never have come to life. If those bright young people had not been funded, half of the splendid reality which exists on the web and which has conquered the planet would not exist today. The companies are almost all American or Anglo-Saxon.

Chapter 16

The Art of Negotiating

At this point I think it is important to introduce some concepts on negotiation, an art that I consider essential in every event of our lives. With colleagues at work, with our partner, with our children, with a car salesman or for other goods. We negotiate, basically, in every moment of our day when we relate to our fellow man, and there is almost always an opposite interest at stake. Negotiation is intertwined in glove with the communication and, according to me, the two disciplines blend during a process that we will call "negotiating". Communicating and negotiating are two skills that can be learned or improved over time: through experience, through study and observation.

My family have always admired me because since I was a child, I had developed a good ability to deal and negotiate. Already at 18, with two of my classmates in high school, I had set up a thriving business of selling used schoolbooks. In the morning we would tour the leading high schools of the city to buy books of the previous year from students who were eager to cash in some money. Then in the afternoon we would sell them at the official market of used books to those parents who wanted to save on the purchase of schoolbooks for their children. Well, we treated with one and with the other generating high revenues with extreme ease. Believe me: I've never had so much money in my pocket as I did then. We were skillful and learned new tricks of the trade every day.

Today, when I buy anything, I have the ability to push the negotiation until I figure out what's the maximum point I can reach and what is the maximum limit at which the other is willing to go. Without ever going too far. It is good for both sides to come out of the bargaining feeling satisfied (you define this a win-win situation). This certainly requires experience, but you can learn and refine your skills.

Negotiation is a challenge, it's a game if you will, where there doesn't have to be a winner and a loser, but where both parties come out more or less winners. Where the skill of the negotiator is to convince the other party that the agreement reached is also to his satisfaction. If everyone thinks of having achieved the best results and comes out satisfied, you maintain good relations and a positive memory, which will come in handy in the future. To conduct a good negotiation, you must also put into practice good communication skills. Let me dwell on the importance of the first impressions: it often affects the whole relationship that follows. A pleasant appearance, not being out of place, show positivity, empathy and motivation will help us a lot. Let's invest some time to prepare the meetings and to imagine what is expected of us. Proper planning, the preparation of a list of things to say and how to say them, will make the difference. Not everyone has the gift of knowing how to improvise and, in a negotiation, there are many obstacles that we may stumble upon. After all we cannot predict what the other party will or won't say and then we may be taken aback. Your appearance, attitude, and action plan are the structure on which to support the content, that is, what we will say to reach the goal.

Communication in a negotiation goes both ways. You must make sure that the other person will listen and perceive your message because that's what counts, really. That's why ensuring your opponent's complete attention is critical. If he is playing with his cell phone while listening to you, I do not think that your message will reach the target. Practice negotiating and face-to-face debates. With anyone. Indeed, the higher the level of your partner, the quicker you will learn. Practice disputing with someone, in predicting and taking apart possible objections. Going into the negotiations as an equal will gives you a confidence that will make you successful. Businessmen are masters of one-on-one debates. Observe others, especially those who you regard as good communicators and good negotiators: you will reap unexpected ideas!

The Basics of Financial Education

I will cite a simple experiment that I feel like sharing also because I have capitalized on it in the past. On several occasions I had to request documents at the town hall and then would go to wait in line at my constituency when I was about 20 years. And because it's in my DNA, I watched and observed the others during the wait. There was an usher (partially disabled) that was directing traffic. He provided information every few seconds; there was a large crowd. Looking at them, I noticed that most of the people addressed him in three ways: most with indifference and coldness; almost all the others with disrespect and distrust; very few with kindness, a smile or a joke. Well, these last obtained valuable tips, shortcuts, help and quickly and successfully resolved their matters. The second category, the one of rude people, spun aimlessly with great difficulty and without resolving anything and, when they returned to the usher with the same attitude, they would obtain similarly incomplete and unclear information. To the remaining group the usher only provided the necessary information, with cold professionalism. The same situation, indeed, even worse, occurred with the employees at the counter, which easily solved the problems or hindered the success of the practices depending the attitude of those who addressed them. From that day forward my behavior at public offices is only one: I stop for a few minutes to observe and understand the situation, then I put on my biggest smile (and maybe a joke) and I turn to the clerk as if he were an old friend with great cordiality, almost creating a complicity. I have never had any more problems. I have obtained ID cards in a day (when usually it took 20), passport with the shortest waiting period, gotten tips, helpful hints, shortcutsand favors unsparingly. And so, when I think, I've done that in my Work towards customers. I do not ask you to believe, but to try, to experience this attitude and then draw your own conclusions.

Companies today are adopting this mode of communication with customers, to improve relationships and to achieve greater results. I have been lucky to exercise a profession which has taught me much in this area and still manages to give me good feelings. Spending time with thousands of customers, colleagues and being in contact with the public, gives anyone who works with business relationship to have a deep understanding of people. Observing various categories, stereotypes and different social classes, leads one to fine-tune his ability to interpret and understand others. And this knowledge leads one to make comparisons. For example: how does your average Joe negotiate? And what about your average Joe pro? Then again each of us has may have asked himself how and what he would do in a situation with this or that public figure, or perhaps a public figure or entrepreneur we admire, and so on. Therefore, through the observation of others comes a spirit of emulation and comparing behaviors, which leads us often adopt an effective behavioural style.

The Basics of Financial Education

Here's a brief list, in my experience, of the winning behaviors to adopt and those to avoid in the business world.

- things to avoid arrogance, self-importance, snobbery and underestimation of your interlocutor. Why poorly predispose one who can help us or one with which we are negotiating an agreement?

- things to be adopted: humility (measured), availability, friendliness. Because these are attitudes that will open up and lower the defenses of the person in front of us relationships that are, as in the case of financial negotiations, always raised to the extreme limit.

In an interview in the first place, it is recommended to open the conversation by softening the tone of your voice, talking about unrelated topics, to get to know each other and break the ice. Then, only after a feeling has established, a relational empathy, can you continue. If you have not created the relationship, moving forward will probably mean the failure of the negotiations, so you might as well try to establish it, before proceeding further. Once you create the right climate and predisposition, go forward with determination, without mincing words, without delay or hesitation to present your own idea of the deal and what terms we want; if the other party agrees, adopt the conclusions reached. The more simplicity, security, transparency we put in our behavior all the more we will appear effective and successful. In the past 50 years loads of texts on behavior, the art of negotiation, relationships and sacred texts on communication have been written. Reading these books, you should know, will always leave you with something positive.

Hard, uncompromising and rough attitudes never lead to anything good. This is also true in relationships between colleagues and family, as well as with friends and acquaintances. Communication is a difficult yet effective art, if properly used. Knowing communication, pnl, the reading of the body signals fine-tunes our ability to be successful. Everything else starts from here. Famous people have made communication their trump card. The smile, sympathy and humor have made the fortune of many average entrepreneurs. The great communicators and leaders captivate crowds with simple behavior and the art of oratory, which is always accompanied by excellent non-verbal communication.

I have learned that in every negotiation and transaction you have to always put yourself in your opponent's shoes to be able to understand his point of view. I invite you to do likewise. Preparing for a business meeting is crucial. If you are unprepared or are thinking of improvising, it is better to postpone the meeting. Being in an inferior position and being surprised can lead to easily succumbing and jeopardizing our plans. How often do we hear every day of foolish things done

The Basics of Financial Education

due to superficiality and misinformation? Let me cite the example of my friend who was duped by a hair loss center because they had convinced him that he was losing his hair...and then he did not know how get out of the onerous contract he had signed (which they didn't force him to sign, he got sucked in voluntarily); another example is that of a dear friend who bought a used car that turned out to be a scam and did not know how to turn back; or that of a relative who was persuaded a financial advisor to make certain investments...and many more !!! I was asked to intervene to solve the problem in all these cases, but maybe they deserved to learn the lesson. I'm sure even you could recount a few stories like these.

In closing I will present my method, which may seem empirical to you, but I assure you has brought me good results. Let me preface this by saying that I am the exact opposite of a stickler. At the same time, I am still extremely handy and I do not like waste time. In my personal things I am extremely pragmatic and synthetic. I prefer synthesis to analysis. Time is money and life. We have little time so let's use it in the best way possible! In this regard, I have developed a way to operate. Take charge and then...action! I have always wanted to know things. I love to go into depth on things that interest me and I'm passionate about. I even study at night until I have perfectly mastered the subject. Then, once I have acquired the greatest knowledge, I step into action. For

The Basics of Financial Education

example, I have become interested in homes, motorcycles, cars and learned all about these arguments, going deeper into details, probing articles, forums, opinions, to formulate a precise idea. Then, I switched to attack mode and made the purchase. Sure, of myself, no second thoughts, sure to do making the best possible purchase. And, surely, without being influenced by anyone (friends, relatives, know-it-alls...). This modus operandi has always accompanied me, and I have applied it in various fields, with great success. In real estate, finance, the art of negotiation, communication etc. etc. But it is also true for the simplest things. Should I buy a vacuum cleaner? I read up on it, but with speed and intensity, so much so that in the end I know more about it than the seller.

This methodology makes us strong, confident, able to talk and deal with anyone. I have experienced many times the feeling and certainty of knowing more than the person selling things. E.g., I am more prepared than a real estate agent when I go to visit a house, or more than the seller or dealer of a car I want to buy. Sellers rarely go in-depth on the models, the engines, the faults or merits of the cars they sell. They do it, with a few exceptions, very superficially and underestimating the buyer. This is something I will advise you do not do. You never know who you have in front of you and in most cases, you will amazed by your interlocutor. Appearance is often deceptive. Everyone often appears as he is not. And the surprises are often unsettling. In the end each of us is made in a certain way but wants to show the world another: hiding fragility, sensitivity, defects and so on.

How many people could you say that, after getting to know them, they confirmed our impression we had at the first meeting? We often fall in love with people who, at first impression, we didn't like at all. The power of conjunctions: "How to win friends and influence people." This is the title of one of the sacred business texts written by Dale Carnegie. A book often poorly translated and not very esthetically appealing, but rich in content. Although dated, I recommend reading it, as you will be left with something. Some concepts have proved very valid in my experience, and I have experienced them in person. Concepts like the one that "confrontation serves no purpose," which when applied to everyday life means that when speaking you should avoid certain negative adverbs or phrases which act on our subconscious directly and make us prepare negatively.

In other publications I have appreciated additional little tips with great utility. In negotiations and communications our subconscious listens and suggests to us what to do. Hearing "no" is, on a subconscious level, a defeat and recalls atavistic memories of when our parents or professors told us "no", "you cannot", "don't do it". Saying to others "no", "but" and "however" is actually an expression of contrast, of not agreeing with the other person. On the other hand if I say "I agree with you...but..however...though...and I express another concept, I am opposing you. You're right... but...I would do it this way. If we try to replace the "not", "but" and "however" with conjunctions, we can still express our opinion without it appearing to be in opposition: "What you say is true...and... I would do in this way"; "I find your vision correct..and...let me tell you mine." That is, I am appreciating and valuing what you say, and I add my opinion, not I am opposing yours. I am confirming what you say (and you are gratified subconsciously) and add and tell you mine like as if it were a continuation of yours, a further specification of your thesis. Although in reality this is not so. So, we agree, we are allies, we are on the same line, the same length wavelength. Try to change your language, you'll have immediate benefits...in your life and at work ...

The Basics of Financial Education

The Basics of Financial Education

About the author

Frank Saro is an european bank manager who has gained a solid experience in various fields, succeeding in combining a global vision of the financial, real estate and business markets. He has had a long career in banking and, before that, worked in finance related and entrepreneurial areas. His passion for real estate had led him to invest in it successfully. He has attended many courses and seminars, also reading books by some of the greatest business authors. Saro's other interests also include communication and NLP (Neuro-linguistic programming) and he believes firmly in the effectiveness of disclosure.

Saro's schooling includes a high school diploma specialized in classical studies, a bachelor's degree in law and a master's degree in computer science. His work experience has been in several fields, including legal, financial and digital, until his entrance in the banking world where he gained experience in five different financial institutions. Today he works for an international banking group and still finds time to follow his passions: writing, studying markets and applying the new technologies to traditional business sectors.

Saro firmly believes that a book can sometimes change our lives and that reading about things that we are passionate about will enrich us more than anything with material worth. He is carrying out his mission to spread his idea of financial education to the general public, which he believes is of utmost importance for each and every citizen.

www.ingramcontent.com/pod-product-compliance
Lightning Source LLC
Chambersburg PA
CBHW070646220526
45466CB00001B/318